Classroom Management

A GUIDEBOOK FOR SUCCESS

Bonnie Williamson

Dynamic Teaching Company
Post Office Box 276711
Sacramento, CA 95827

CLASSROOM MANAGEMENT: A GUIDEBOOK FOR SUCCESS
By Bonnie Williamson

Published by: Dynamic Teaching Company
                 Post Office Box 276711
                 Sacramento, CA 95827
                 Telephone: (916) 351-1912
                 Fax Orders: (916) 985-7832

Copyright © 1992 by Bonnie Williamson

Printed in the United States of America

Cover and book design: Robert Howard Graphic Design

Editors: Marilyn Pribus
            Kathy Hoff

Illustrations: Dale Crawford

Typesetting: Pauline Howard

Library of Congress cataloging in Publication Data

Williamson, Bonnie
        Classroom Management: A Guidebook for Success
        Includes resources and index

1. Classroom organization
2. Education, elementary classroom
3. Discipline, elementary classroom

I. Title

Library of Congress Catalog Number 91-077578
ISBN 0-937899-15-1

To Marie Van Dyke
who took the time to teach me the "HIP way."

OTHER BOOKS BY BONNIE WILLIAMSON

A First-Year Teacher's Guidebook for Success
(1988)

101 Ways to Put Pizazz into Your Teaching
(1991)

REVISION

A number of teachers and bookstore owners over the past two years have requested that I incorporate additional information into my original book, *How to Organize and Run a Successful Classroom*. For this reason, I've rewritten extensively, changed the title to reflect the changes, added more information for intermediate teachers and included more than a hundred illustrations and a section of Teacher Resources.

ACKNOWLEDGEMENTS

First, I thank Lynn Pribus for her patient help and continual encouragement in editing this book. She reinforced for me the positive motivating effect of "earning points." Also, Kathy Hoff, for her outstanding patience in making sure that every comma, hyphen and quotation mark was correct.

I also thank Donna Von Rajes for her input for primary teachers and Robin Chacon for allowing me to spend time observing her intermediate classroom. I particularly wish to thank the parents who rallied behind me in my classroom as I field-tested the "Honor Incentive Point (HIP) method."

Bonnie Williamson
Sacramento, CA
1992

CONTENTS

Chapter 1	*Here's a Bright Idea that Really Works*	1
Chapter 2	*Get Ready...Get Set...Go!*	5
Chapter 3	*The Five Big Rules*	11
Chapter 4	*Points Pay Off*	23
Chapter 5	*The Payoff*	33
Chapter 6	*Job Meetings*	43
Chapter 7	*Class President*	49
Chapter 8	*Class Meetings: Primary*	57
Chapter 9	*Class Meetings: Intermediate*	65
Chapter 10	*Discipline Procedures*	71
Chapter 11	*Kicking Toward Success*	79
Chapter 12	*Station Breaks*	83
Chapter 13	*Time Out*	91
Chapter 14	*Reaching for the Stars*	101
Chapter 15	*Time and Money Management*	105
Chapter 16	*Reactions to HIP*	113
Chapter 17	*Questions and Answers*	119
Teacher Resources		129
Index		132

1

Here's a Bright Idea that Really Works

*C*indy is a first-year teacher. Her third-grade classroom abounds with students who constantly misbehave. She's not sure she can stick out the year.

Harvey has taught for five years. He has used several different types of discipline programs in his classroom with so-so success. Next September he will be moving from second to fifth grade and he wants to find a new classroom management system — one that works.

Ramona has six years of experience. She teaches second grade and is tired of her room arranged in the traditional manner with six straight rows of desks. This year her school will begin using the "Total Language Program" and she wants her students to be able to work in groups.

These are just three of the many teachers who are seeking a better way to manage their classrooms.

THE HONOR INCENTIVE POINT (HIP) SYSTEM

Whether you are 23 or 53, a beginning teacher or one who has taught thirty years, sooner or later, I predict you will ask, "What can I do so I can teach more and discipline less?"

After twenty years in the classroom, reading a variety of books, attending workshops and employing many different discipline methods with my students, I was still not fully satisfied with the results.

One year, however, things were different. My split class of second/third graders won awards at the Science Fair, was honored for reading many books and frequently received a trophy for being the best-behaved class in the school cafeteria.

I was also rewarded. I received my highest evaluation ever, excellent in every area of my teaching and classroom management. My classroom became a "showplace" for exhibiting excellence in education to student teachers, substitutes, and inquiring parents.

What was my secret? I had begun using a classroom management system I learned from Marie Van Dyke, a remarkable thirty-year veteran of the elementary school classroom. Mrs. Van Dyke had attended San Francisco State College as an elementary education major and during her final year in college, she was selected to be a student teacher at Peralta School, a prestigious teacher-training institution in Oakland, California.

Many of her classroom management and organization skills came from Peralta and her supervisors there. Through the years she has added her own ideas, developing her successful Honor Incentive Point (HIP) system-approach to classroom management.

Today parents ask to have their children in Mrs. Van Dyke's classroom while the youngsters are still in nursery school. Student teachers are eager to be placed in her room because of her reputation as an outstanding teacher and disciplinarian.

About a year before I started this new system, I asked Mrs. Van Dyke to be my personal HIP mentor. I visited her classroom and took notes as she marked points on the chalkboard, conducted Class Meetings and then presided over the Job Meeting (all part of the HIP system), and we spent hours talking about her successful HIP classroom.

I then used the HIP system in my own room. Along with the system, I incorporated a number of my own successful teaching techniques. Many of these ideas appear in the next fifteen chapters as HIP TIPS.

Why does this method work? What is the secret? Simply, the system is an effective, workable partnership between the teacher and students.

Peer persuasion, rather than teacher coercion, is the main focus of HIP. The teacher serves as Chairman of the Board and also, at times, as a judge or facilitator, but mostly as a supportive leader in the classroom. The system works because it allows you, the teacher, to join with students in a *shared* responsibility for a classroom where learning takes place.

Classroom Management: A Guidebook for Success is a step-by-step guide demonstrating how to use the Honor Incentive Program (HIP), a classroom recipe book to guide, give tips and point the way to success in classroom management.

The HIP system provides you with the power to get your students to do what you want them to do, yet it is not a dictatorial management style. Instead, it is a democratic process of classroom involvement between students and teachers where the dominant atmosphere is one of interpersonal respect.

Each person is part of a community in a HIP classroom where the teacher, the student and their parents all work together for the benefit of the group, as well as for individuals. The children learn how to be cooperative citizens in the democratic setting of their own classroom. The system is simple and easy to implement; most of all, *it works*.

In the HIP classroom, elections are held, jobs are gained through the voting process and discipline is maintained through peer pressure, leaving teachers to do what they do best — teach!

It was exciting for me to field-test HIP for two years and see the procedures in this book come to life. Although I successfully used the HIP method for two years, I'm no longer able to use its principles. Four years ago my inner-city principal asked me to set up and run the computer lab for the school. Since my classes change every thirty minutes, I do not use the system now but if I should go back to the classroom, I will. I am confident that those who read and apply these techniques in their own rooms will also see positive changes.

2

Get Ready . . . Get Set . . . Go!

During the spring, many schools hold what they call "Play Day" or "Field Day." Students look forward to this release from the classroom with joyful glee while many teachers pray the day will soon be over!

Still most of these Play Days turn out to be resoundingly successful. Why? Because hours of preparation have gone into planning the activities, soliciting parent volunteers and getting the equipment organized.

It's every bit as essential to be well organized in the classroom, but rather than planning for one day, you must have overall goals for the entire year. You must preplan for success. How do you begin to do this?

ROOM ARRANGEMENT

The HIP system is based upon arranging the room into "stations." A station is a group of desks placed together. Throughout the book my basic classroom will use desks divided into three stations.

Here's how it would work. Arrange the three stations in the shape of a "U." On the left side of the "U" place five desks spaced at least twelve inches apart. Behind these, stagger six desks so each student in the back row has a clear view of the front of the room. If space in back is a problem, place six desks in front and five in back.

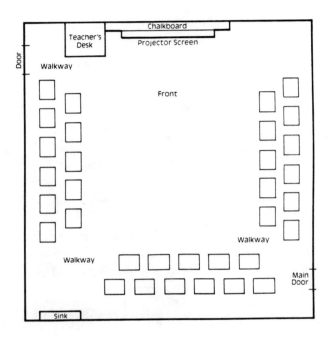

HIP STATION ARRANGEMENT

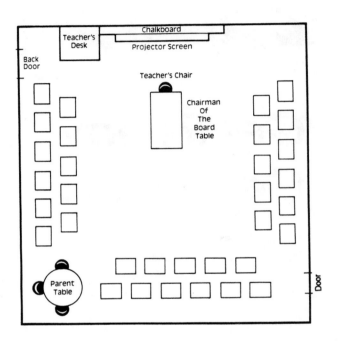

CHAIRMAN-OF-THE-BOARD TABLE

Repeat the arrangement with eleven more desks at the "bottom" of the "U"; then move on to the right side of the "U" and space the remaining eleven desks.

Place your own desk to one side in front of the room. Be sure to position it to provide an unobstructed view of you and the chalkboard.

COOPERATIVE LEARNING AND TOTAL LANGUAGE DESK ARRANGEMENTS

More and more teachers are using the Cooperative Learning method for teaching in their classrooms. Briefly, Cooperative Learning is students working together in heterogeneous groups. Usually this means students are grouped into stations of four or five desks. Each group should consist of high-, average-and low-achieving students with a mix of boys and girls and be racially balanced as well.

Also as more school classrooms move toward Total Language where students no longer use a reading textbook but read and write from a variety of literature books, students also need to work in small groups.

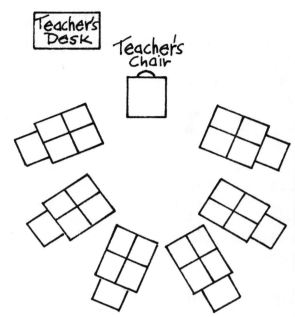

HINT: Begin in September with the HIP three-station arrangement. By October you should know your students' academic strengths and their behavior problems. You then can arrange the students so they work as two separate groups within a single station while maintaining the station identity for purposes of the HIP program.

In fact, it isn't essential to have exactly three stations within a classroom. You could easily use this method with five or six stations. This would be the arrangement to use for Cooperative Learning.

HOW TO CONVERT THE STATION ARRANGEMENT TO SMALL GROUPS

It's easy to turn a HIP classroom into a small-group setting. At the beginning of the year, list names on the chalkboard so students will know their groups. Also, let them know exactly where each group will work. This will enable them to move their desks and chairs quickly without causing the move to be a major project.

HIP TIP: Schedule your small-group learning for the time just after recess or lunch, but have your students move into place beforehand. Then when you return to the classroom, they will be ready to go to work.

Train your students to move, one group at a time, into their Cooperative Learning positions. You might use signals for this. When the first group is in place, have the second group move and then the third. Vary the order from day-to-day.

HIP TIP: There are several ways to gain students' attention, depending upon their grade level. Some examples are standing with one arm raised, sounding a note on a piano if one is available or switching the lights on and off. A small bell with a melodic sound works particularly well.

Use the same plan in reverse to have students move back into their stations.

CHAIRMAN OF THE BOARD

In big corporations one room is designated "The Board Room." Instead of having your board members seated around the table, they are spaced around the outside of the "U."

As teacher or chairman of the 31-member board, you need a special table which will be as important to you in the next ten months as to any Chairman of the Board.

Ask your principal for a rectangular table about six feet long and three feet wide. Place the table lengthwise in the center of the "U" with your own special chair at the head of the table about three to four feet away from the chalkboard, which is behind you. See drawing on page 6.

THE CHAIRMAN'S ACCESSORIES

Not only must a chairman have a Chairman-of-the-Board table but also accessories such as pen, pad and perhaps a gavel to gain attention and make meetings run smoothly. You, too, need specific items nearby to make the day pass in an orderly manner for you and for your students.

It is also important to make the room colorful and attractive. Pick out a bright place mat and put it in the middle of the table. Place three baskets and a colorful coffee mug or jar on the mat.

Keep a fresh supply of sharpened pencils in the mug. Ask students to place broken pencils in one large basket before taking a fresh pencil. In another basket (pick a different color) keep a supply of crayons, erasers or whatever extra items you want to have available for those with missing supplies. The types of materials you keep in the baskets will depend upon your grade level.

The third basket should hold slips of paper for jotting messages, ballots for voting and for writing notes or spelling words for students, as needed.

HIP TIP: By keeping supplies such as pencils, crayons and erasers on the "Chairman-of-the-Board" table, you cut out many potential behavior problems. When supplies are in the back of the room, you invite students to loiter, argue over the longest pencil and spend valuable minutes digging through a bucket of supplies looking for the "perfect eraser" while missing an entire spelling test.

Depending on how you operate your room, you may keep your lesson plans on your regular desk or on your table. Since you will spend more of your day at the table, keeping the lesson plans there can save minutes and footwork.

PARENT TABLE

When parents take the time from their busy schedules to help in the classroom, it is important to create an area where they can sit quietly and observe, grade papers or listen to students read or repeat their multiplication tables. Find a sturdy table and several chairs which can be placed in the back of the room for their use. If you cannot locate such a table at school, look around at garage sales for something suitable at a fair price.

KINDERGARTEN HIP CLASSROOM

Even five-year-olds enjoy the experience of being in a HIP classroom and you'll discover that many methods used in the regular 1-6 HIP classroom can be adapted to a kindergarten setting. See the illustration for a kindergarten classroom using Bear stations.

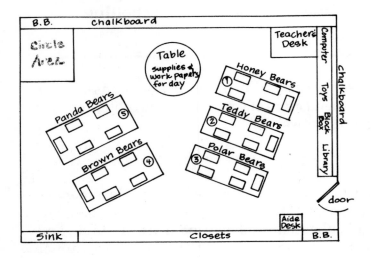

Instead of using the chalkboard for keeping track of points, you may wish to use a large magnetic board. On the left side, list the names of the stations. Instead of chalk marks, design animal paws and attach magnets to the backs.

During the day when a station receives a point, put up a paw next to the name of the station. Put up another paw as more points are accumulated. However, if a station loses points, turn one paw around going backwards (or remove it entirely) to indicate that one point will be removed.

Depending upon where you teach, you may need only three stations, or in some classrooms five or six. In a number of kindergarten classrooms in the East, seventeen is the usual number of students. In California that number grows to thirty-two, which is the maximum number allowed by law.

HIP TIP: Kindergarten teachers have discovered it is much easier to get students to clean up after snack time, put toys away and line up when using the HIP method.

Now that you have your room arranged, you will discover how important written rules and oral directions are. You are going to learn how YOU can run a successful classroom.

3

The Five Big Rules

Most students come to school knowing about "home rules." The majority of them have a specific bedtime, for instance, rules about doing homework before watching television and other rules of behavior in the house.

Use these "home rules" as a foundation for establishing classroom rules. Spend time on the very first day of school talking about "our classroom family." During the next two or three days, mention the need for rules in a family, especially one with many children and only one adult. Discuss the need to set up rules to make it fair for everyone in the room, including the teacher.

For example, you might lead the students into a discussion of how it feels to be called "stupid." Ask students if they have ever been called names. Spend time talking as a group about the feelings you get when you are called bad, vulgar names. Do these words make you feel glad? Sad? Do you want to hit someone for calling you names?

ROLE PLAYING

It is important when discussing feelings to use more than words to illustrate what happens inside people when they are called bad names. Role playing allows students not only to hear but also to see these feelings on someone's face when others are rude.

Tell the students you are going to play some games which will help them understand how important it is to think of others' feelings.

Here is an example:

> Boy 1 played by Ramon
> Boy 2 played by Dewayne
> Teacher played by Mr. Scott

Teacher takes the boys outside the room and tells them how he wants them to role-play their parts. Mr. Scott, Ramon and Dewayne return to the classroom.

> *Mr. Scott:* "Ramon, you were telling me you took a trip to Yellowstone National Park this summer. What did you enjoy most about the park?"
>
> Before Ramon can answer, Dewayne yells out from across the room: "That's a dumb place to go. I went there last year and it's..."

Mr. Scott: "Ramon, how did you feel about not having time to answer the question I asked, and how did it feel to have Dewayne say you went to a "dumb place?"

Ramon: "I felt sad and hurt that Dewayne would yell out when I was trying to talk and then say Yellowstone was a dumb place to go. I loved it there. I wanted to tell the class about the mother bear and two baby cubs I saw but Dewayne wouldn't let me."

Mr. Scott: "Class, do you see how Dewayne's yelling out and not giving Ramon time to answer was wrong? It took away Ramon's ability to give the answer he wanted to share. Class, how did Ramon's face look when Dewayne yelled out at him?"

Spend several minutes letting students talk about this situation and how they might feel.

Mr. Scott: "Dewayne, now I want you to look at Ramon and say, 'I'm sorry, Ramon.' "

Dewayne apologizes.

Mr. Scott: "Class, do you think we need a rule about talking out so this won't happen again in our class?"

Help the class discuss the wording for a rule. When they agree on a specific rule about talking out in the classroom, have the students vote. Then write the rule on the chalkboard.

HIP TIP: After the vote about talking out in class, take a moment to go over the right times to talk in class. Example: raise your hand, wait until the teacher recognizes you, then talk.

Now select two girls to illustrate how students should not behave in the classroom, again explaining in private how to play their roles. Have Phong Le stick her foot out in the aisle and trip Amy as she walks to the drinking fountain.

Mr. Scott: "Amy, how did you feel when Phong Le tripped you and made you fall against Mark's desk?"

Amy: "Awful! I felt silly and stupid and angry that Phong Le would do that to me."

Mr. Scott: "Phong Le, why did you do that to Amy?"

Phong Le: "Because she wouldn't pick me to be on her soccer team at lunch yesterday."

Mr. Scott: "Phong Le, that is not the way we treat classmates in this room. You also need to understand that Amy could have been hurt when you tripped her. I want you to apologize to Amy now."

Phong Le: "I'm sorry I treated you that way, Amy."

Again lead the class into a discussion of why we need to have particular rules and how much more harmony we have in a classroom when we all obey the rules.

In the next few days, continue to role play and discuss the types of rules needed in the classroom.

You cannot simply write the rules on the chalkboard the first day of school or talk about your classroom procedures only the first week. This must be ongoing.

HIP TIP: Here are five successful ways to implement rules and procedures:

1. **Clearly define the rules and routines so your students understand what is expected.**
2. **Teach the rules and procedures. Write this as a lesson into your lesson plans the first month of school.**
3. **Observe your students' behavior to be sure they are correctly following class rules and procedures.**
4. **Be prompt and consistent when you see students misbehave.**
5. **When a problem starts to develop, step in before it escalates.**

After a number of rules have been presented, have your class talk about and vote on them. Those with the most votes are written on the chalkboard. Each Friday erase the rules and every Monday have your students help you rewrite them on the chalkboard. During the opening month of school, go over the rules daily. Later, review them only on Mondays or when a new student enters the classroom.

SELECTING THE RULES

Depending upon the age and the needs of your students, the number and type of rules will vary. Older students' rules will have a different wording from those for first graders. Intermediate students may also need a few more than primary students.

Caution: Do not overload your class with too many rules. Make a few and make them direct and to the point.

HIP TIP: It is vital that students have a say in the choice of rules, or they will have little meaning for them. Based upon the role-playing exercises, lead students to understand how rules help protect our rights, make us responsible for our actions and help build self-esteem and confidence in being a good citizen not only at school, but in the home and in the neighborhood.

PRIMARY CLASSROOM RULES

Here are the rules which one primary class finally settled upon. Although they are typical rules, your class may use different words.

1. *LISTEN*. In order to learn and get smarter, students must listen to their teacher, to other students and to the lessons as they are presented.

2. ***WORK WELL.*** This means that students should try to do their very best work at school. Working well means getting smarter and feeling good about oneself. It is reflected in good grades.

3. ***KNOW WHEN TO TALK.*** Students coming back to school after summer vacation are used to talking whenever they please. In order to learn, they need times when they do not talk. At other times it is important to talk and participate in class discussions. (This is when to decide if you want the students to raise their hands before talking).

4. ***KNOW WHEN TO USE YOUR HANDS AND FEET.*** Kicking, shoving and hitting are ongoing problems. Students need to understand that each of them can come to school without fear of being hurt. Discuss again the "our family" concept of treating each other with respect. This rule will remind students not to bother others. Then draw the class into a discussion about using hands and feet at the right times such as playing on the playground and using hands for writing, asking to talk and doing art work.

5. ***REPORTING.*** Countless valuable minutes are lost when students tattle. Talk about the precious time spent away from learning. Explain to the class about "Reporting" which means a student should come to the teacher only to say that a child has been hurt or is ill. All other problems must wait until the Class Meeting. See Chapter 8.

INTERMEDIATE CLASSROOM RULES

In the intermediate grades, it is important to set aside a period of time early in the school year to decide upon classroom rules. Here are some which were used in an outstanding intermediate classroom and can serve as a guideline.

1. Follow all directions.
2. Complete your assignments.
3. Ask for permission to leave the classroom.
4. Be an independent worker.
5. Always keep your hands, feet and objects to yourself.

RESPONSIBILITY FOR LEARNING

We need to help students understand *they* are responsible for their learning. One way of doing this is to point out that the best learning takes place when students are listening, following along in the textbook and actively taking part in class discussions.

In each class I've had since the day I started teaching, at least three students (and sometimes more!) had no idea why they were in school and no intention of learning. Instead, they sat, played and passed notes to others. These students are likely to become dropouts later.

In order to help forestall this, we need to make these failure-prone students aware of their choice to fail while they are still in elementary school.

For an outstanding book on how to motivate students to learn, see page 129 in Teacher Resources.

GRAPHING

One visual way to help students grasp their responsibility in school is to frequently draw graphs illustrating success and failure. During the first week of school it is important to draw a "Success/Failure" graph each day. Then throughout the year, as needed, draw a graph and discuss the choices students have to become smart students or failures.

Use your chalkboard or overhead projector with colorful pens to do this. Draw a large rectangle on the board or overhead and place the days (Monday, Tuesday, Wednesday, etc.) with the dates underneath: Sept. 4th, Sept. 5th, etc. On the left side of the rectangle write the numbers 0, 10, 20, 30, and...100 from the bottom up to the top.

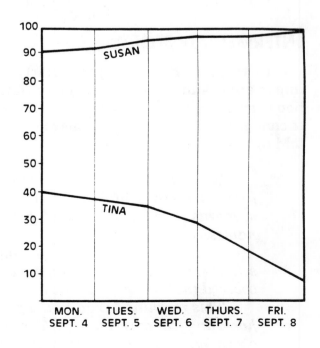

THE SUCCESS/FAILURE GRAPH

In the primary classroom tell about two students in another school. Call these students by any name except for the names in your classroom. Example: Susan and Tina.

Explain to the class that Susan pays attention in class, does her homework and is interested in getting smart this year. Say: "Look at the green line I'm drawing. Susan began school on Monday by doing her math and reading and she starts out making 90% on the first day. The next day she gave an oral book report and she is now up to 95% in her grades." Show that by Friday, Susan will be making 100% in school.

Now tell the class about Tina. Explain that Tina brings toys to school and hides them in her desk so she can play with them. She also spends her time looking around the room and not listening to the teacher. When she moves into her group work, she pays little attention and lets others on the team do her work. She also forgets to take home her homework and she is often tardy and misses part of reading several days a week.

Draw a red line for Tina showing she only did half her math and got 40% the first day. Since she missed reading the second day she got zero, and by the end of the week she was spending most of the day playing with things in her desk. She ended up with a zero grade for the week in most subjects.

Explain to the class that what this means is that Tina does not care. She *chooses* not to be smart.

Then ask the students which line they would like to represent them — the green or the red. Ask, "Which line do you *choose*?" Explain again that the choice is up to them.

Each day vary the graph using different names and some days talking mostly about behavior choices. Illustrate on the graph what happens when poor behavior keeps students from learning and interferes with making good grades.

Follow each graphing lesson with a few minutes of open discussion.

INTERMEDIATE STORY

In the upper grades, particularly when teaching fifth and sixth grades, it is important to state again and again the importance of an education. This can be brought home graphically by telling a true story from your teaching experience. You may wish to change the names and locations or you may decide to "tell it like it is." Here is the story told by one sixth grade teacher.

Several years ago I had a sixth grader I'll call Ricky. He was often late for school or absent. When he did come, he never had his homework and spent his time fooling around, bothering other students and calling them names.

I tried to get him to see the importance of an education yet he said school did not mean anything to him. I followed Ricky's progress and discovered that in eighth grade he dropped out of school and got into drugs.

This morning I read in the paper that he had broken into someone's home and was carrying out a TV set when the police caught him. He pulled a gun but the police shot first and killed him. Ricky was only sixteen years old.

Students, do you see the importance of an education? If Ricky had stayed in school and worked hard, he could have accomplished a great deal. He was a smart boy, but he made a dumb choice. Although he had outstanding ability, he simply did not care. I want you to know that I care about you and I want you to care about yourself and your future.

I'm here to help you have a bright one.

One way to help reluctant students in intermediate grades want to achieve in school is to devise a successful seating arrangement within the classroom. Peer pressure is very important and you need to use it to bring out the best in your students.

One method which works well is to seat a popular, academically minded girl next to a boy who fools around. He will look up to the girl and will have next to him an outstanding example of a good student.

On the other hand, place a girl who goofs off next to one of the more popular, smart boys in the classroom. His energy and enthusiasm will rub off on her and she will emulate him.

Another way to reinforce the idea that being smart is a choice is to use a daily greeting as a reminder to students that they come to school for a purpose: to learn.

PRIMARY OPENING

In the primary room, this greeting ceremony or "catechism" might be like this:

Teacher:	"Good morning, boys and girls."
Students:	"Good morning, Mr. Scott."
Teacher:	"Why did you come to school today?"
Students:	"To get smarter."
Teacher:	"Why did Mr. Scott come to school today?"
Students:	"To help me get smarter."
Teacher:	"How many teachers do we have in our room today?" (When parents are helping they should be included in the count).
Students:	"Two."
Teacher:	"How many students do we have in the room?"
Students:	"Thirty-one."
Teacher:	"And that is why we have rules in our room. Tell me rule number one." (Teacher walks to the chalkboard and points to it and the students read all the rules in unison).

Do the greeting in its entirety as needed to remind students about the rules and being smarter. At other times, only go over the initial greeting to where the students say, "To get smarter." You'll find this a great way to begin each day.

INTERMEDIATE OPENING

In the intermediate classroom, the opening will vary, depending upon class and teacher. The Flag Salute is frequently the first order of business.

Important notices for the day are announced by the class president. This is sometimes followed by a word search, students writing in their daily journals if your class uses them, or an oral math problem to be solved by the group.

HIP TIP: By having your students write in a journal each day, you enhance their creative writing skills. You can let them write whatever they wish for five or ten minutes or ask them to answer a question. This might be: "What is your favorite flavor of ice cream and why?" Or, "What kind of clothes do you most enjoy wearing?" Take a few minutes each day to write brief comments about what they have written in their daily journal folders to keep their enthusiasm going.

You might also consider collecting brief, inspiring stories from a newspaper or television program, especially about unusual achievements by students the same age as yours. Have a different student read one aloud each day.

In this chapter we have talked about the importance of rules, classroom procedures, seating arrangements and staying in school. We have also addressed various ways to begin each day, depending upon the grade level.

In the next chapter you will see how "earning points" can be a positive and highly motivating experience for students in your successful classroom.

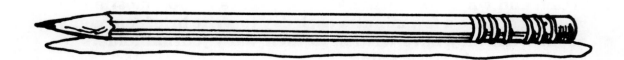

4

Points Pay Off

Children have a natural interest in competing whether on the playground, in a spelling bee or seeing who can get to their seats first. This competitive spirit makes the HIP system function well day after day and month after month in the classroom.

The method centers around the stations in the room. Here is an effective way to begin the first day of school. As the students come into the room, ask them to remain at the back. Explain that you are not going to assign seats to them. This will come as a happy surprise to most of them. Invite them to look over the room and decide where they would like to sit. Assure them that they can choose a seat by a friend in one of the stations and as long as they behave properly, they can sit in the seat they have selected. However, they must remember that if they talk or do not pay attention, you will move them.

Ask them to walk quietly to the seat they would like. If two students want the same desk, they will need to negotiate and you may need to help them settle the matter. Later in the day, post their names on their desks. I found it best to write names on sentence strips and cover the strips with an overhanging piece of Contact ® paper. Place the name on the front of each student's desk where it will remain until the last day of school.

The students may then remove the name tags and take them home as souvenirs of the year. This works very well, particularly in the primary grades. In the intermediate grades, name tags on desks are not always used except for the first few weeks of school.

HIP TIP: Many teacher bookstores now carry commercial seating signs which you may purchase. However, they are small. They stand about two inches high and are six inches long. They have the "- - - - -" line as a guide for upper and lower case letters. Also you can purchase some without the middle guide line. The signs are made with stands so each name tag stands on top of a student's desk.

The students remain at their chosen desks all year except for the president and vice president. See Chapter 7. However, after the first week if certain seating combinations selected by students do not work out, you must move them. You'll also want to monitor stations all year to be sure none is ever overloaded with discipline problems. Problem students should be divided among all the stations.

Always keep one unused desk available in one station with necessary supplies ready for a new student. This empty desk can also serve as a barrier between two students who need to have space between them. When a new student arrives, the desk is ready and waiting — a nice sort of welcome. Immediately obtain another empty desk to repeat the process, usually placing it in another station.

There may not be an equal number of students in the stations but this does not present any problems.

HIP TIP: Especially in fast-growing areas, extra desks and chairs are hard to find. Be persistent. Go to your custodian and ask him for a desk. He likely will tell you he has none. Then ask if you could look over his "junk pile" of old desks and chairs. Often, desks needing only a few repairs are in the heap. Pick out the best one and ask him to fix it for you when he has time. Also, bringing him a plate of fresh homemade cookies once in a while helps!

Naming the Stations

As the day school begins, discuss with the class the manner in which the desks are arranged. Use the word "station," and ask a student to look up the definition in the dictionary and read it to the class. Follow this by explaining to the students that each station will need a name. This can be done during the first week by ballot within each station. Again the students should take part, under the guidance of the teacher, in this process.

Here is how one primary classroom chose their names.

In a discussion led by the teacher, the students began to talk about the positions of their stations in the classroom. It soon became apparent that the three stations were arranged on the north side of the room, the south and the west. One student even brought in a compass to verify the locations and the students unanimously decided to call themselves "North," "South" and "West" stations.

The station names should be easy to say and only a word or two in length because they will be used constantly during the year. Here are a few more ideas: Use a patriotic theme such as "Red, White and Blue." Also, names of trees, animals and football teams.

At the intermediate level, you may wish to appoint a committee to bring suggestions to the group or seek nominations from the floor. Names such as football teams, rock groups and rap artists are frequently requested by students.

After the selection, the names are printed in the most prominent place on the chalkboard. Explain to the class that each station can earn points by good behavior, following directions and participating in classroom activities. Also, stress that messing around, not following directions and disrupting the class can result in a loss of points for a

HONOR POINT CHART

station. Tell the students the points will remain on the chalkboard all week in full view of any visitors coming into the room.

HIP TIP: It is vital to begin the point system as soon as the station names are listed on the chalkboard. Example: After the recess you might say, "I like the quiet way each station walked into the classroom after recess this morning. Each station earned five points."

Immediately encourage the class to applaud their good work in earning their points. I used clapping a great deal during the day to reinforce the positive feelings that come from earning points. Here is how we did our "Three-Clap":

> *Teacher counts:* "One, two, three"
> Class: One giant clap
> *Teacher counts:* "One, two, three"
> Class: One giant clap
> *Teacher counts:* "One, two, three"
> Class: One final giant clap

By counting and doing one single clap together, you foil students who clap on and on trying to be silly. This also takes care of the student who always wants to be the last one to make a noise when clapping. This method works well and gives students the thrill of competing to see if they can all end at the same instant. A variation, especially for older students, is to substitute finger snapping for clapping.

A new point count is begun on the chalkboard each Monday and continues through Friday dismissal.

HIP TIP: Use the addition and subtraction of points as a way of teaching math facts. Students enjoy vocally helping the teacher add or subtract points to their stations' chart totals. They are especially delighted to assist the teacher as she or he subtracts points from a rival station. When an addition or subtraction mistake is made, at least one station will let you know of the error in a most resounding manner!

WAYS TO EARN POINTS

When any adult walked into my room, be it parent, the nurse or counselor, and said to me, "My, but you have a fine class," each station automatically earned five points. When the principal said "great class," the stations each earned ten points. The points were added just as soon as the guest left the room. I explained to the class what the guest said and how proud I was of them. After I added the points to the totals, we all clapped or snapped our fingers.

Stations can also earn points by being the first cleaned up and with all students sitting quietly when it is time to go out to recess or P.E. or when they walk in quietly and settle down to work.

When students leave the classroom and your control, you can emphasize good behavior by telling them they can still earn points. Take, for example, a trip to the library for their weekly lesson given by the school librarian. You can tell them as they walk out the door that when you pick them up a half hour later, you will add twenty-five points to each station's total if no names from their station appear on the library chalkboard. However, if you note, for example, Jason's name on the chalkboard from North Station, then that station will not earn their twenty-five points.

This also works very well when taking a class to an assembly. Remind them you have a notebook and will write down names of misbehaving students. This helps to keep problem students in line. I've had teachers say to me after an assembly program, "Your students were so well-behaved in the assembly this morning." As soon as we returned to the classroom, I passed this information on to the class; we clapped and added points to each station's total.

HIP TIP: When your students leave your room, always walk them to their destination. This is a good-neighbor policy to use and shows respect for all the classes around you. DO NOT open the door and let your students dash to the library, for example. On the way, they will fight, hide out in bathrooms and roar into the library, upsetting the teacher who must then take a long time to settle them down. Do the same for recess and lunch. Other teachers will appreciate your thoughtfulness.

The HIP program is not designed to be a "teacher-controlled discipline plan." Instead, the system functions whether the teacher is in the room or not since the peer pressure continues to operate.

The peer system also works when a substitute arrives in your classroom. In my top desk drawer was a bright red folder marked "HIP TIPS for Subs," including how to add and subtract points from the stations. The students were well aware than even when I was away from the classroom, they were still able to earn extra points by continuing to behave well.

Tell the class that if you return and find the substitute has had a good day in the class, each station will receive a substantial number of points — thirty, for example. However, if even one student from a station misbehaved so much that the name is noted on the sub's report, that station earns no points.

Students also become creative in thinking of ways to earn points. One boy returned from recess with a $5.00 bill he had found. After sending the money to the office, I had the boy stand with me in the front of the room while we did our "Three-Clap" and then his station received twenty points for having such an honest student.

Another boy, I noted, frequently stayed after school when his station needed points. Without my saying a word, he cleaned all the chalk trays, dusted the erasers outside (not on the wall of the building) and put out chalk. When he finished, he casually walked up to me and said, "Mrs. Williamson, tomorrow morning could I remind you of what I did so my station can get an extra ten points?"

HIP TIP: When students are more restless, such as before and after a holiday like Halloween, before vacations or on windy days, be very generous with points.

FOUR ADDITIONAL WAYS TO EARN POINTS

You can be very creative in ways students may earn points. It is indeed rewarding to see how hard they work in order to earn points for their stations.

The point system is a fantastic way to get things from home. Here are some examples:

- Five points for each station member who brought in a milk carton when we made ice cream in our room. For information on how to make individual ice cream servings in your classroom see page 129 in Teacher Resources.
- Five points to each station for students who brought in an embroidery hoop we needed for an art project.
- Five points for each person in a station who brought back their signed report card.
- Ten points to a station for any student whose parents attended one of our special class programs.

Points should be awarded the first thing in the morning for those bringing things. Students are quick to remind you to get to the board and get the points recorded. Only the teacher can add or take away points from the total.

Following opening morning activities, move to the chalkboard to see which station is ahead. Example: West Station. Ask those students in West Station who brought back their report cards to raise their hands. Collect the cards and count them and multiply the number by five and add this to the total score for West Station; then call upon the other stations. Totalling points in the morning should not take more than three or four minutes.

HIP TIP: Bad news does not travel well by hand. Invest in extra stamps and mail to parents such negative news as Deficiency Notices or notes regarding poor behavior. When the student returns the signed note to you, reward his or her station with extra points.

POINT REMOVAL

Points can also be subtracted from a station's score. Example: If during a math lesson, you look up from the overhead projector and see that a girl in South Station is slipping a note to her neighbor, you say, "Someone in South Station is writing notes and not listening, so I must take a point away from her station."

If that same girl continues to write notes, use her name saying, "Cassandra is continuing to write notes and not paying attention, so she is choosing to lose another point for South Station."

You want students at that station to let Cassandra know that she let them down. They may turn around and say quietly, "Oh, Cassandra," but they cannot yell out, "OH, CASSANDRA!" for then you take off another point.

Points may also be removed when a station's students run into the room and make noise. Immediately say, "North Station was being too loud today; they chose to lose five points." Stations can lose points when a student fools around and holds up the class from getting started on a lesson or project. Points are also deducted when a student throws something or gets angry and swears at a classmate.

POINT REWARDS

Students quickly learn that the station with the most points gets a big payoff. Here are some examples:

- Any treats, such as cupcakes brought for celebrating birthdays, go first to the station with the most points.
- The station with the most points goes out first for recess and lunch.

- During an art project, the station with the most points is first to select paper and drawing materials.
- The station with the most points gets the choice of seats on the school bus on a field trip.
- Most important of all, students in the station with the most points on Friday afternoon at dismissal time get to pick all the classroom jobs they want for the following week.
- In the intermediate grades, the payoffs may differ, depending upon your students and what kind of payoff they want.

HIP TIP: Before you leave on Friday afternoon, be sure to record the station with the most points in your Lesson Plan book so you won't forget.

In the next chapter you will discover why choosing classroom jobs is the BIG PRIZE at the Monday morning Job Meeting, particularly in the primary grades. Intermediate teachers will discover good motivators for their students as well.

5

The Payoff

FEB.

MONDAY

*B*oys and girls look forward to Halloween, Valentine's Day and the day before summer vacation. HIP students look forward to Mondays as well.

The heart of the HIP system is the payoff. In primary grades it is the Monday morning Job Meeting at which the students at the station with the most points for the previous week choose the job assignments for this week. (Each station begins anew each Monday and works hard to try to be the winner for that week.) Intermediate classes may use jobs or other payoffs.

It is important to have a job for each student in a station. Only students in the winning station are ever eligible for jobs in the primary classroom; otherwise, you defeat the purpose of the HIP System. If you have only five or six students in a station, then you would have only that many jobs unless students want to do two jobs.

HIP TIP: As soon as you walk into the classroom on Monday morning, go to the chalkboard, write "Honor Points" and underneath, list the names of the stations. Then check your Lesson Plan book for the winning station from Friday. If North Station won, draw a star next to North Station. The star will save you many minutes during the opening morning activities since the students will know who won.

Here are some examples of typical jobs. Again remember how important it is to have input from students. You may be surprised at what they feel needs to be done in your classroom. Later, having had a voice, they will energetically take part in keeping the room in good order.

JOBS IN A PRIMARY CLASSROOM

The president and vice president are the most important officers in the classroom. Their jobs will be discussed in Chapter 7.

Bailiff: The bailiff serves in place of the teacher for recording points when the teacher is occupied with talking to parents in the room, for example, or carrying on a Class Meeting. See Chapter 8.

If a problem develops while the teacher is busy, the teacher will say, "Bailiff, someone in South Station just threw an eraser. Please go to the board and take off five points."

While the teacher conducts the Class Meeting, the bailiff sits in a chair underneath the Honor Points chart and adds or subtracts points at the teacher's direction. *Only the teacher ever changes the totals.*

CHANGING POINTS ON THE
HONOR POINT CHART

Paper monitor: This popular job involves passing out all paper to each station during the week. The student may distribute the paper individually to each student or select a person at each station to hand out papers. This position gives the student power in choosing special people to be the passers and is eagerly sought after.

Light monitor: This job also gives the student a feeling of importance. The light monitor tends the lights for films, sometimes inserts and removes the cord for the overhead projector and turns lights off and on when coming and going for recess and lunch break.

HIP TIP: Present a five-minute lesson to your students on the correct way to remove electrical plugs from wall outlets. Most will grab the cord in the middle and yank till the plug pops out. Show them how to grasp the plug close to the outlet and gently remove it. This will save you much time from having ripped cords repaired or replaced.

Curtain monitor: This student opens and closes the drapes for movies and for the overhead projector, as needed.

P.E. equipment monitor: This job is considered a most important position by students. The monitor is responsible for taking out P.E. equipment as designated by the teacher for recess, lunch and during the P.E. period. The monitor picks a boy and girl each time to be in charge of the equipment on recess and lunch period.

The following jobs are best done at specific times of the day: for instance, the Flag Salute is done the first thing in the morning. It is often best for the teacher to designate a specific time for the sink person and librarian to perform their jobs when they will not distract students from classwork. Often these jobs tend to get noisy and can disturb others around them who are working. The only need for change would be if the student assigned to the task is absent. In that case the teacher selects the president, vice president, or volunteer to fill in.

Flag monitor: The flag monitor walks forward, gives the "Stand, salute, and pledge" directions and remains standing in the front until the class finishes saying the Pledge and sings "America."

Class librarian: This person makes sure the class library is neat and tidy.

Sink person: The sink and drainboard are kept clean by this student.

Closet person: The chosen student makes sure the closet area is kept neat at all times during the day.

Sweeper: Five minutes before going home, the sweeper cleans the rug in the classroom. This student particularly enjoys being able to say to messy students, "Please get that stuff cleaned up under your desk so I can sweep."

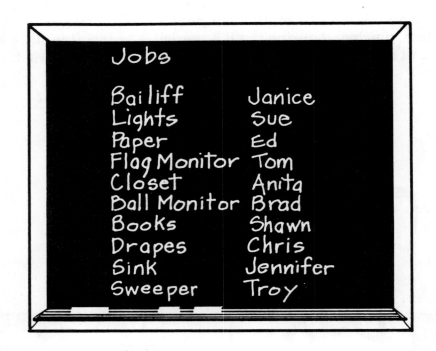

JOB CHART IN HIP CLASSROOM

HIP TIP: Give yourself a present if you do not have a rug in your classroom. Get one! After twenty years of noisy footsteps, dropped objects and scraping metal chairs and desks day after day, I decided I deserved a rug. I purchased two widths of inexpensive carpeting, and two fathers helped me put it down. We used carpet tape underneath to secure the rug to the floor. I then used duct tape around the edges to stick the carpeting down. Be sure to clear this in advance with your principal, because your district may have rules about having all carpets sprayed with fire retardant first. The morning after we installed the carpet, three mothers walked in to help me. They stopped, listened and smiled. One said to me, "Oh, it is so quiet in here. What a difference!" I wished I'd put down carpeting twenty years before!

Of course, your classroom may need different job classifications, and while some of these jobs are necessary in an intermediate room, the increased maturity of the students makes other, more responsible jobs suitable as well.

KINDERGARTEN JOBS

A president, vice president and bailiff can be used in a kindergarten room. All other jobs can be determined by the teacher. Their jobs can be patterned after those in the primary grades depending upon the abilities of a given kindergarten class.

INTERMEDIATE JOBS

You may wish to award jobs to the winning station each week in your intermediate classroom using the method from the primary. In this case all jobs would be awarded to the station with the most points at 3 p.m. on Fridays.

In addition to classroom jobs for the winning station, here are some additional motivators which have worked well in intermediate classrooms:

- One fifth/sixth-grade teacher arranged to have the winning station go to the computer room for thirty extra minutes each Friday. Students worked very hard for this privilege.

- A sixth-grade teacher provided additional P.E. time for the winning station each week.
- A fourth-grade teacher arranged for the winning station to be in charge of the "Student Store" each week where they sold cookies, pencils and erasers. Play money was used and went into the winning station's bank account to be used to buy items from the store, extra free time or to go out to lunch with the teacher.

TOTAL-CLASSROOM HIP METHOD

While field testing the HIP program in the intermediate grades, some teachers discovered that their students would not buy into the primary single-station job program. A total-classroom-committee method was used instead with great success.

When using this method, the entire class works together as one big station to earn points and the payoff will benefit the entire class.

A typical payoff could be seeing a video each Friday if the goal is reached.

HIP TIP: You should preview the tape before the Friday showing. In fact, you may have a "short list" of videos from which the class may choose.

Total classrooms might also vote to bring in tapes and be able to listen to "their music" during the day. This can be done all day or at special times. This choice might need to be negotiated.

Others might decide to have a party on Fridays, complete with popcorn and soft drinks.

Depending upon your class and your situation, you'll need to decide before the opening of school which plan would work best for you.

You also might choose to use one payoff one semester and change to another the following. Be flexible. If one payoff ceases to work, try another.

COMMITTEES AS THE PAYOFF

Another effective way to involve the whole classroom is through the use of committees. With this plan, the teacher assigns students to head committees to do the jobs. This method is done from a class roster so each student should have an opportunity to serve as a committee chairperson during the year.

Prior to selecting committees the teacher and the class must decide how many points the entire class should earn in order to receive a payoff.

Here are some suggestions for committees: The teacher each month selects the committee chairpersons. Each chairperson selects his or her committee members from the class. This can be done orally, by ballot or by the chairperson going privately to students and requesting they serve. You'll need to discuss the method which would work best in your classroom. The most important goal is that each student be given an opportunity to serve either as a chairperson or be on several committees during the year. Here is how the chart might look on the chalkboard:

COMMITTEE CHAIRPERSONS
OCTOBER

Art	Sara
P.E.	Roger
Library	Phong
Bulletin Boards	Dale
Paper	Ramon
Computer	Michele

Art committee: This group develops art projects for the month based upon the teacher's lesson plans. They get all materials ready for the project each week.

P.E. committee: These students decide upon the P.E. activities for the month. It is also their responsibility to have all equipment in good condition and have it out on the playground at the proper time.

Library committee: Students work with the teacher to gather books which go along with the lessons for each month. They go to the school library and check out books, reference materials and pictures which will help to research the topics to be studied.

Bulletin board committee: These boys and girls work closely with the Art committee. They are responsible for designing all the bulletin boards for the month. They post art projects and other pictures which they obtain from the library committee. They also must be sure that all materials are returned to the right students and the library committee at the end of the month.

Paper committee: This group is responsible for all paper which will be used in the classroom each month. They check to be sure all needed paper and art materials are ready to use and pass supplies out at the appropriate time.

Computer committee: These students work closely with the classroom teacher and the computer resource teacher (if one is available). If the class is doing a unit on a certain topic, for example, the committee lets the computer teacher know ahead of time. They also schedule times for various students to go to the computer lab to work with the encyclopedia. (Many schools are now purchasing an entire encyclopedia on disks to be used as a reference, particularly in the intermediate grades.) For example, if students are working on an article on earthquakes, they would notify the computer lab teacher what topic was needed and sign up for an available time slot.

Each intermediate classroom is different and teachers will need to decide what is most helpful in their own classrooms.

HIP TIP: No matter whether you are teaching primary or intermediate classes, you must have enough jobs for each student within a station. No student should ever feel left out. If you have five or six students in a station, you need to have at least five or six jobs. If you have more jobs to do in the room than station members, ask if some would be willing to do two jobs.

The idea of using play money at the intermediate level is something else you might consider. It motivates students to work hard, mind rules and keep up homework.

One fifth-grade teacher uses a weekly auction to improve classroom discipline. He collects coupons from local burger shops as well as used games and other white elephants from friends. The students also bring in items they wish to put in the auction. When students line up correctly, behave well in class and obey classroom rules the teacher pays them a specific amount of play money to be used at the weekly auction. The students look forward to this period each week and work hard for the opportunity to bid on favorite items.

Be aware that problems do arise even when using play money. Students may steal from each other, so you should urge them to take the money home until the day of the auction. Another solution might be to provide a bank with officers chosen from the classroom.

Another teacher uses the point system but instead of Monday jobs, she lets her sixth graders select field trips — often out of town. By earning a specific number of points, the class may go on trips they choose. Her particular school has additional funding which helps defray some costs. If your school does not have extra funding, read Chapter 15 for ways you can raise money.

In this chapter you've learned how important it is to have a payoff in the classroom to induce students to "buy into" your behavior management system. In the next chapter you'll learn how to conduct a Job Meeting in the primary and intermediate grades.

6

Job
Meetings

*B*y the third Monday of school you should introduce the Job Meeting to your students. In the primary grades, jobs are the HIP payoff. Intermediate students often prefer committee jobs and want other payoffs like field trips or special class privileges.

JOB MEETINGS IN THE PRIMARY GRADES

All primary jobs go to the winning station — the one with the most points at the close of school on Friday. A classroom can have three, four or even five stations. But only one is the winner each week. Then on Monday morning, congratulate the winning station for doing a fantastic job and lead a Three-Clap to let them know you and their classmates recognize they are winners.

Though students may nominate each other, some want a particular job. The meeting often goes more smoothly if they can nominate themselves.

Mrs. Smith: "Is there anyone in North Station who would like to nominate themselves or someone else to be the bailiff for this week?"

Janice (standing): "Mrs. Smith, I would like to nominate myself this week to be bailiff."

Mrs. Smith: "Thank you, Janice. I'm recording your nomination."

Then perhaps one or two other students will make nominations. Record each of these names.

Mrs. Smith: "Does anyone else in North Station have a nomination for bailiff? If not, we will vote. Will Janice, Phong, Eric, Linda and Brandon put their heads on their desks and close their eyes. Everyone else in class please stand."

HIP TIP: By having the students stand for the voting and then sit down after casting their vote, you can be almost sure no student votes twice.

Mrs. Smith: "Remember, students, you may vote for yourself. Now, will all those students who wish to have Janice as your bailiff, please raise your hands?"

After the teacher counts and records this information, the students who voted for Janice sit down. Continue in this manner until all those nominated have had their votes recorded. Even if no student is still standing, call out the remaining names so no one feels left out.

Mrs. Smith congratulates the student elected, invites student applause and walks over to the chalkboard to write the title "Jobs" at the top and "Save" after the title so no one will erase this until Friday dismissal.

Underneath "Jobs" she writes "Bailiff — Janice."

Bailiff	
Janice	9
Phong	5
Brandon	4
Eric	4
Linda	3

The primary meeting continues until all jobs have been taken — normally about thirty minutes. Keep in mind that some students may not want a job or if the job they want is already taken, they may choose to sit out the remainder of the meeting without trying for another.

HIP TIP: Some students from the winning station might be absent or out of the room on Monday when the meeting is held. Remind your students that they should ask someone in their station to nominate them if they cannot attend the meeting. The student should give the friend a first and second choice of jobs he or she would like.

Job Meetings in Intermediate Grades

In the intermediate classroom, you may use the same job set-up as at the primary level. However, this may not be as effective for older children. You may wish to use a committee system instead.

If the entire intermediate class is working toward some BIG event on Friday, then all students become eligible for the jobs or committees.

In some classrooms the teacher prefers to select committee chairpersons from a class list and check off their names as they serve. This way all students will have a turn as chairperson during the year. In other rooms, the teacher decides to have students vote for the chairperson of their choice.

HIP TIP: Be sure you keep an accurate checklist of those who have served as chairpersons and those who have served on specific committees. Each student should have the opportunity to serve on as many committees as possible. Also, you may need a rule that one person cannot serve more than once or twice as chairperson. This ensures that all students will have a chance to take part.

	ART	P.E.	Bulletin Board	
Alan	✓			chair
Brittany			✓	
Corey		✓		
José		chair		✓
Sara	✓			
Phong			✓	

If you decide to use the committee approach, you'll want to hold your Job Meeting on the first Monday of each month. However the chairperson is chosen, it is then his or her responsibility to pick two or three others to serve on the committee. This is a real motivation to be able to select friends to work together.

It is best to have the committee serve for one full month. Even with input from the teacher, committees such as art and P.E. need longer than a week to decide upon activities for the month. The P.E. committee needs to work out a schedule which will enable the class to challenge other classes, for example, in baseball, volleyball or basketball. They need to meet for a planning session within the first three days of the month and later at the discretion of the chairperson.

If you wish to have the students vote for chairpersons, photocopy a blank ballot ahead of time. Students can enter the names of nominees to head each committee as they are nominated. The person with the most votes becomes the chairperson.

No matter what method you use for chairperson selection in the intermediate grades, one of the finest payoffs is seeing the democratic process in action. When students take on responsibility for running their classroom, their interest remains high and the responsibility enhances self-esteem.

HIP CHART

Even while the committees are functioning, you still have your HIP chart on the chalkboard. For example, if it has been decided that the class must earn 200 points to listen to music tapes on Friday, then you will credit points for walking in quietly, behaving well in assemblies and for cooperating with substitutes. You'll also deduct points when students break classroom rules.

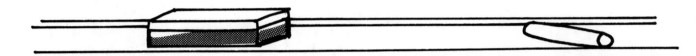

The Warriors
Points needed $\overset{1}{2}\overset{9}{\cancel{0}}\overset{1}{\cancel{0}}$
Friday-We have -152
$\overline{48}$

If the class falls short of the goal, then no music tapes will be allowed on that Friday. Instead, provide time on Friday to review the rules and hold a Class Meeting to find out how the class can work together to achieve the goal for the next Friday payoff. Begin again with a clean chart on Monday and remind your students to work hard toward the class goal.

In this chapter you've learned how to conduct the Job Meeting and how to form committees. In our next chapter you'll discover the importance of having a president and vice president in the HIP classroom.

7

Class President

*F*ootball fans sitting in the stands hold up giant gloves with an enlarged index finger boasting their team is number one. Auto manufacturers tout their car as the number-one automobile sold in the country. Car rental agencies compete yearly to be able to claim, "We're Number One." Being number one brings status, clout and name recognition to the winner.

Primary Presidential Election

Each month in the HIP classroom, one student is elected president and another vice president, the number-one-and-two status positions. Students eagerly look forward to entering the competition to be class leaders.

Prior to the first election, it is important to spend time talking to the students about elections and how they are run in our country. Discuss the Democratic and Republican parties and how several candidates run for the Office of President every four years although only one is elected.

Spend time discussing how a person inspires others to vote for him or her. Your students need to see the value in being friendly, kind and outgoing so classmates will know them. As the teacher, you are already aware that certain students stand out. These exceptional boys and girls exhibit leadership qualities and the ability to talk in front of a group. Usually they are popular among their classmates. But all students need to know that anyone can run for class president and anyone can win.

HIP TIP: At the beginning of the school year talk about the shy, quiet student who seldom speaks out as opposed to the disruptive or problem-maker student. Encourage your quiet students by saying, "I know you're just as talented as the others in the room but we don't know you. I want you to begin to make friends, be friendly and 'let your light shine.'"

Also address problem students who, due to poor behavior, are unpopular in the classroom. These students need to understand that their *behavior* keeps them from being the type of persons others want in leadership positions. Encourage problem students to become the type of friends others respect, admire and choose to nominate for president.

PREPARING FOR THE PRIMARY PRESIDENTIAL ELECTION

Here are some important facts your students need to know before you conduct the first presidential election:

- The election will always be held the first Monday of the month just prior to the Job Meeting.
- The winning station from the previous week nominates candidates, or members of the winning station can nominate themselves.
- When nominated, a candidate must then pick a running mate who can be *from any station in the classroom.*
- After votes are counted, the presidential team will be the team with the most votes. If several teams tie, hold a runoff election.

This election is conducted in a slightly different way from the Job Meeting to give the presidential election more honor, more ceremony befitting a presidential candidate.

HINT: After you and your students have gone through a couple of these elections, the entire selection process should not take more than ten to fifteen minutes.

PRESIDENTIAL AND VICE PRESIDENTIAL MOVES

Following the election, the president and vice president will move to specially designated seats, even if this means they leave their current stations. The newly elected president will sit near the main door and the new vice president near the other door.

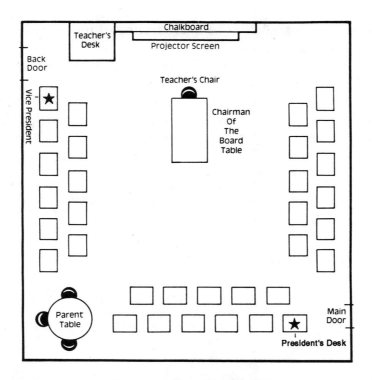

SEATING PLAN FOR PRESIDENT AND VICE PRESIDENT

HIP TIP: Use the movement of president and vice president at the first of the month as a natural time, if needed, to move a misbehaving student or two out of a station and into the new president or vice president's vacated chair. One of the "retiring" class officers can then take the trouble maker's seat. This can be done without seeming to point out any one student as being a problem.

PRESIDENTIAL AND VICE PRESIDENTIAL RESPONSIBILITIES

At the first presidential election, explain to the class what the president's and vice president's duties include. Here are some presidential responsibilities from a typical classroom:

- The president answers all knocks at the main door and escorts guests into the classroom.
- The president conducts "Telling the News," and "Tell Time" in the primary grades and "Sharing" at the intermediate level. See Chapter 12 for explanations of these activities.

- The president leads the class to a prearranged meeting place outside for all fire drills and alarms.
- The president becomes the line leader for the entire month so will always be first in line going out and coming in.
- The president delivers messages to the office for the teacher.
- The president serves as a substitute for any absent student who holds a job such as the flag monitor or the sweeper.

Here are the responsibilities for the vice president:

- During a fire or fire drill, if the main door is blocked, the vice president leads the class through his door and to the designated meeting place outside.
- At all other times, the vice president is the last person leaving the classroom, making sure everyone has left so the teacher can lock the door.
- The vice president is the last one in line when returning to the class room from recess and lunch and seeks to get all stragglers into line when the bell rings.
- The vice president takes over when the president is absent.

INTERMEDIATE PRESIDENTIAL RESPONSIBILITIES

At the intermediate level, the president holds a more responsible job with more decision-making power than at the primary level.

Here are the duties of a president in an intermediate classroom:

1. Conduct Sharing each day or several times a week.
2. Be in charge of Class Meetings while the teacher serves as a facilitator. In some classrooms the class president is in charge of conducting the meetings.
3. Meet with the various committee chairpersons in the classroom as needed to clarify duties of each group.

MODELING PRESIDENTIAL JOBS

Prior to a presidential election, you must model what you wish the president and vice president to do. This should be done during the opening month of school.

During the first month of school, you'll conduct Sharing for about ten minutes each day or if time is not available on a daily basis, at least three times a week. Sit in front of the class and look at the HIP board to see which group is ahead. Begin with this station by asking if anyone has something to share.

HIP TIP: This is an excellent time to have students give brief oral reports on science projects, health lessons or social science units. Sharing time is a more relaxed part of the day to give a report than a specific time during science, for example. Many students will be doing the same thing and no one student need stand out and feel uncomfortable. The same is true if your students are working in Cooperative Learning groups and several from each group will be presenting reports.

At the intermediate level, students may wish to share from a broad range of activities going on in their lives. Some might tell about a musical group they are forming while others bring in hobby-related items and share with the class the enjoyment they receive from various leisure activities.

CLASS MEETING

If the president is a good leader, he or she can often chair the Class Meeting. If possible, conduct this important meeting at least twice a week. Schedule a regular day and time such as every Tuesday and Friday at 12:40 p.m. after the lunch recess.

In the intermediate grades the president (or teacher) does not serve as judge and jury. Intermediate students instead give suggestions to those asking for help. The president or teacher, serves as a facilitator. For more information on Class Meetings see Chapters 8 and 9 and Teacher Resources, page 129.

VICE PRESIDENT

As in the primary grades, the vice president fills in for the president in leading Sharing, Class Meetings and working with committees.

INTERMEDIATE PRESIDENTIAL ELECTION

The election should take place at the beginning of the second month of school after all students have had an opportunity to watch the teacher model the roles of president and vice president.

In the intermediate grades, any student may nominate candidates for president and vice president. Then, rather than using a show of hands, have the students vote on slips of paper which are folded and dropped into a basket. The students receiving the most votes for the offices become president and vice president for the coming month.

HIP TIP: The teacher should carefully select three students to count the votes. These should be students who can be trusted to count ballots and keep the results confidential. The teacher should warn that no one else is to know the number of votes for the candidates. This information should be kept private to avoid hurt feelings.

Again, as in the primary levels, have the president and vice president sit in designated seats. Each month after the new president and vice president are elected, move not only the former officers to another seat but also students who are behavior problems. All students should know that unless they settle down, they might be moved the first of the month.

In this chapter you have learned the importance and prestige value of the positions held by the president and vice president in the classroom and how to hold a presidential election.

In the next chapter you're going to learn how to conduct a Class Meeting in your successful primary classroom.

8

Class Meetings: Primary

*E*very teacher finds that where there are students, there are complaints. Here are some typical examples:

> Paul cannot find the new baseball glove he brought to school for Telling the News. He tells his teacher he saw Mike, a classmate, with a glove exactly like his at recess.
>
> Sixth-grader Phil complains to his teacher that while playing soccer, Doug, a fellow student, deliberately kicked him.
>
> Amy, a second grader, says to her teacher, "Mark threw food across the table at me in the cafeteria and it's the third time this week."

In order to teach in a successful HIP classroom, you need to arrange a time to listen to the complaints which frequently arise. The Class Meeting provides such a time.

CLASS MEETINGS

What is a Class Meeting? Who are the leaders? When should a Class Meeting be held?

A Class Meeting in the primary grades is a carefully controlled, teacher-directed activity. This is a time set aside each day when children can get their gripes out in the open. Most of the time, their complaints center around the way they are treated by fellow students. At this age they are quick to bring up problems involving other classmates.

Students are aware they are not to tattle, yet some always will. The teacher must quietly, but firmly say, "Bring it up at Class Meeting today." To help students remember, as you write the rules on the chalkboard each Monday, remind them not to come to you and tattle. Take time to specifically talk about "Reporting" only which means when someone is hurt or ill, they need to let you know. All other complaints and problems will be addressed at Class Meetings.

HIP TIP: The timing of the Class Meeting is important. If at all possible, conduct it during the last fifteen minutes of the day when departure provides a natural ending to the meeting. If your class is on the early-late reading schedule, for example, hold the meeting just before early students go home. Normally, fifteen minutes is sufficient time for a Class Meeting. If more problems than usual arise during a particular day, or the agenda is full, allow extra time. Sometimes, though, when the timer rings, some students will object, "But, I didn't get my turn." You can observe, "Tomorrow if you work harder, perhaps your station will have the most points and you'll start Class Meeting."

PLANNING AHEAD FOR CLASS MEETINGS

At the beginning of the school year, decide how many Class Meetings you'll have each week and when. Write this down in your Lesson Plan book. During the first week of school introduce the idea of weekly Class Meetings and take time to tell your students what to expect.

Continue teaching your students the rules and procedures for a Class Meeting for at least ten minutes three times a week as part of your daily lesson plan. Many students have never been involved before and will naturally be nervous about what is expected of them.

HOW TO CONDUCT A CLASS MEETING IN A PRIMARY CLASSROOM

Begin by ringing the bell or alerting the students in some way that Class Meeting will begin in a few minutes. Students need to clear their desks and be sitting quietly before the meeting begins so that all students can be heard, even those with soft voices.

HIP TIP: If students are slow to settle down, find one station ready to begin. Example: If it is West Station, say, "West, you are doing great. Your station is quiet and ready for Class Meeting. You've just earned ten points." This will get the other stations' attention in a hurry.

Sit at the Chairman-of-the-Board table. The bailiff should be sitting near the Honor Point chart to deduct points as you direct for misbehaving students.

Ask the bailiff which station is ahead. If it is South Station, as an example, say, "Does anyone in South Station have a compliment to share in Class Meeting today?"

Allow two or three minutes at the beginning of each Class Meeting for students to give compliments to each other. This begins the meeting on a positive note. Example: Sarah says, "I want to thank Cheryl for helping in the cafeteria today when my lunch bag broke," or Tom says, "I would like to thank Andy for coaching me at soccer this morning."

After the compliments, ask for problems which need to be discussed. Have pencil and paper available and take brief notes on students' names, a few words describing the problem and the stations involved.

HIP TIP: Provide yourself with a timer. If you expect the Class Meeting to last about twenty minutes, set the timer to ring in fifteen minutes. This will alert you, if you're in the midst of settling a major problem, that it is time to end the meeting. Always allow an extra few minutes after the timer rings to get the students ready and out the door.

A typical example of a Class Meeting problem would be when Amy is unhappy because someone threw food at her in the cafeteria. Amy is not permitted to give the offending student's name; instead, the food thrower is first given the opportunity to admit to the act.

Amy raises her hand. When she is recognized, she stands and explains to Mrs. Williams and the class that someone in North Station threw food at her.

Mrs. Williams: "North Station, Amy tells me that someone in your station was breaking a cafeteria rule by throwing food today. Will that someone please stand up?"

Sometimes the student involved will stand immediately, but not often. Wait a few moments to see if someone will stand. Then look at Amy and say, "Will you tell me who threw food at you today?"

Amy: "Mark did. It's the third time this week and I told him I was going to bring it up at Class Meeting today."

Mrs. Williams: "How did it make you feel, Amy, to have Mark throw food at you?"

Amy: "I felt really sad 'cause he messed up my new blouse and sort of mad, too, 'cause he got food in my hair."

Mrs. Williams: "Mark, please stand. Did you throw food at Amy this week?"

Mark: "Yes."

Tell Mark how disappointed you are in his behavior and explain how he made Amy feel bad. Then ask him to apologize to Amy. Wait a moment for Mark to look at Amy and say, "I'm sorry."

The majority of students are satisfied when someone apologizes for a minor offense but with more serious incidents an apology isn't enough.

STUDENTS WHO HURT OTHERS

When students hit, kick and threaten to beat up other students, you must take a firmer approach. The offending student needs to understand that he or she has done something very serious and will be held personally responsible.

In cases where students hurt others, it works well to ask the injured students to suggest some form of punishment for the offenders. With the Perimeter rule built into the HIP system, this is usually the punishment suggested and works well. For more information on the ladder of discipline, including the use of the Perimeter in a HIP classroom, see Chapters 10 and 11.

As these more serious issues arise, it is wise to have the class vote on what should be done as punishment. The student creating the problem must be made to realize that his or her behavior is wrong and is unacceptable to fellow classmates.

Here is an example: If one of your students grabs the yard stick off the chalk tray and hits the child next to him, say, "Stephen, why did you hit Ralph and put yourself on the Perimeter?"

Between student peer pressure and your words, these misbehaving students should become fully aware that they are performing unacceptable acts which must stop.

HIP TIP: I once had a student who refused to apologize to anyone in the classroom. I could have put the Class Meeting on "hold" till June and the student still would refuse to say, "I'm sorry." I had the class take a vote about what we should do with Ron. They voted that he had to walk the Perimeter the next day and miss P.E. Sometimes this was enough to make him say the magic words; other times he chose to walk the Perimeter. At a parent conference, his mother told me, "The kid has been stubborn since the day he was born." I then understood. This tip shows that not all problems will be solved.

CLASS MEETINGS BENEFIT PRIMARY STUDENTS

How do Class Meetings help students? Why is it so important to take fifteen or twenty minutes out of a busy day for another meeting? What does this type of meeting teach students?

First of all, the Class Meeting gives students a forum to present their problems or concerns before the teacher and the class.

Another important point of extreme interest to the student is that not only will a problem be heard, but retribution of some kind will be meted out. In this process, students see democracy in action.

Students discover during Class Meetings that their problems are important, that they themselves are valued and their point of view carries weight. All of this builds self-esteem in their lives.

Students also quickly learn through Class Meetings that their bodies are sacred. No one has a right to call them names, or to hit or kick them. If this should happen during the day, they can be heard at the Class Meeting forum and punishment will be swift for the guilty party.

HIP TIP: Many students will come during the day complaining that three terrible things happened that they must present at the Class Meeting. However, this would make the Class Meeting much too long. Instead say, "I'm sure all three are important, but you'll have to pick the most important one to bring up." This helps students gain skills at making decisions.

ROLE OF THE TEACHER IN THE PRIMARY CLASS MEETING

More than anything else the teacher serves as a model of how our judicial system works. Students learn what is right and what is wrong.

The teacher acts in the role of judge in the classroom and the no-nonsense Class Meeting is highly structured with a rigid format. The very same procedure is followed day after day with the only change being that the station with the most points leads off.

Students see that the teacher/judge listens and sometimes asks for more information from other students involved before making a decision.

HIP TIP: Don't let students stand up in Class Meeting and recite the vulgar names they were called. This can set off a giggling session. Instead, ask the student to come up and whisper the word in your ear. This will take a lot of the emotion out of the incident while letting you determine if the word was really bad or just something silly.

The teacher should certainly let his or her feelings show during Class Meeting. A teacher says in a sad voice, "Brian, I cannot believe you would call Sharon such an unpleasant name. That makes me sad." Students need to hear genuine emotion in a teacher's voice when they misbehave. These emotions can range from mild shock to shock to visible distress that anyone in the class would do such a thing. Students need to see how their actions can cause others harm.

On occasion, the teacher invites input from other students, and children are asked to produce witnesses, if needed, to prove their point. In other words, the teacher must be willing to take the time to clearly understand what happened.

HIP TIP: If time runs out, and someone didn't get to report a problem and is still very upset, take the child aside for a moment and listen to the problem. Often, a listening ear is enough and by tomorrow the crisis will be forgotten.

Some aspects of Class Meetings are similar for primary and intermediate grades. However, older students have different problems, and in the next chapter you'll see how to conduct a Class Meeting in an intermediate classroom.

9

Class Meetings: Intermediate

*I*n the intermediate grades, small incidents in the classroom and on the playground can escalate into major problems. Often students no longer resort to mere name-calling or "tattling" but use their fists to get their message across.

Problems frequently involve relationships between boys and girls and teacher and students; they sometimes even escalate to include threats upon fellow students.

In order to cope with this daily barrage of insults and threats, it is vital that you conduct a Class Meeting. By getting problems out in the open, you can often prevent an escalation of the grievance. As always, some students will want to complain to you about other students. Simply direct them, "Write it on the Class Meeting agenda."

Remind students about "Reporting." That is, when someone is ill or hurt you need to know. All other problems will be addressed at Class Meetings. Giving students the opportunity to be heard can defuse a situation. In the end, you'll benefit by setting aside time each day or several times a week for a Class Meeting. Paradoxically, you'll have more time to teach.

Older students are much more capable of understanding cause and effect, boy-and-girl relationships and they are eager to seek a solution to problems. In fact, you may choose to train the class president to conduct the meetings while you sit nearby to offer guidance when needed.

During a Class Meeting, you will serve as a facilitator, demonstrating how the democratic process is used to solve problems. You'll want to ask questions such as, "How do you feel about this?" "What do you think we should do?" "Why do you suppose Eric did that?" Or, "How could we help Mi Lee feel better today?"

FOUR REASONS WHY CHILDREN MISBEHAVE

In the book *Maintaining Sanity in the Classroom* by Dreikurs, Pepper and Grunwalk, four reasons for "mistaken behavior" are addressed. See page 129 in Teacher Resources. They occur when a child seeks:

- To get attention
- To demonstrate being powerful
- To get revenge
- To make others think he or she can't do anything right so as to reinforce his or her own feelings of inadequacy

When you are aware of these four common reasons for misbehaving, you can address them during the Class Meeting and help your students to better understand themselves and others. You should also guide the students to an understanding of "logical consequences" and show them how to distinguish between a consequence and a punishment. A consequence is a logical result of an action, while a punishment is a penalty which is imposed for misdeeds.

During the meeting the teacher should read the students' suggestions such as: "Eric should apologize" or "Ramon should have to write 500 sentences for cussing out Marcus." The students can determine which ones are logical (suitable) and the ones which are punitive. The punitive suggestions should be eliminated because they are not helpful. Soon the students themselves will understand the difference between consequences and punishment.

HIP TIP: To cut down on verbal interrupts, introduce the class to "hand signals." During a discussion, a student who agrees with what a classmate is saying can give a "yea" which means moving the lower arm slowly up and down without speaking. To register a "nay," it should be moved back and forth horizontally.

PREPARING FOR THE CLASS MEETING

When it is time to start the intermediate Class Meeting, use a prearranged signal to alert students to stop whatever they are doing and get ready. This might be turning the lights off and on, ringing a bell, snapping your fingers or simply saying, "It's time for Class Meeting."

One of the best methods for getting students in these grades to participate in the Class Meeting is to have them move their chairs into a circle.

Ask two or three students at a time to bring their chairs to the designated area. Otherwise, the movement can turn into a pushing and shoving match with chairs. Instead, always begin the meeting in an orderly manner.

It is advisable at this age level to have an agenda. A notebook with a pencil attached to a string inside a binder is ideal. If students need to bring up something at the Class Meeting, they can write their name and a brief description of the problem in the book. This should not be done during class but rather during recess, lunch or before or after school. This will cut out minor gripes since students must give up part of their "free" time to write out the complaint.

It is important that all Class Meetings begin with compliments. The meeting begins on a positive note and students can see that this is not just another "gripe" session. It also helps students focus on the good in others. Some students are not comfortable giving compliments so you'll need to model this frequently during the first month of school. Explain to your students that you are teaching them how to give compliments and that you are sincere when you give them. For example, you might say, "I appreciate the way both Tony and April volunteered to help Mr. Lopez move his science exhibits into the multipurpose room for the parent meeting tonight."

INTERMEDIATE CLASS MEETING RULES AND PROCEDURES

Meetings are held so everyone can work together to solve problems and help each other. This means teacher and students must practice mutual respect. It includes listening to others and taking turns. The basic meeting structure is this: When a problem is introduced at the Class Meeting, the student who entered it in the agenda tells the class exactly what the problem is.

- Ask those involved if the problem still exists.
- The student or students involved are asked what the logical consequences should be.
- If the student or students do not recall their part in the incident, the teacher asks witnessing students for clarification. When students get to the intermediate level, names are used from the beginning in Class Meetings.
- Once the class decides the person was involved, consequences are discussed and voted upon.
- Each student then has an opportunity to give his or her reaction to the consequences. After reactions, deal with the next item on the agenda.

A SAMPLE INTERMEDIATE CLASS MEETING

Ms. Hing walks over to her desk and picks up the agenda binder.

Ms. Hing: "Does anyone in the group have a compliment today?" Several of the students say something nice about other students in the classroom. For example, "I want to thank Ross for helping me with my decimals after school last night. Now I finally 'get' how they work."

Ms. Hing reviews the agenda for items not previously marked out as having been settled.

Ms. Hing: "Jason, three days ago you wrote that Russell had been making funny remarks about your new haircut. Have you two settled this yet?"

Jason: "Yes, we talked it over during recess and he isn't going to kid me anymore."

Ms. Hing draws a line through this complaint and goes on to the next.

Ms. Hing: "Sarah, you wrote that Stacey had been writing notes that were not true about you and a boy in this class. Has this been settled yet?"

Sarah: "No, it has not. She is still doing it and I want it brought up today."

Ms. Hing: "Sarah, please explain what is going on."

Sarah says Stacey has been sending notes around in class saying that Sarah met with Zack after school behind the gym. Sarah explains that she did see Zack but only to ask him to have his sister call her because she needed help with her Social Studies paper.

Most arms go up and down in agreement.

Ms. Hing makes notes on a piece of paper regarding information given.

Ms. Hing: "Any comments?"

Josh: "I overheard their conversation and that was what she was asking Zack." More hands go up and down in agreement.

Students vote that Stacey should apologize to Sarah. The teacher then asks for any other tips for Stacey.

Kathy: "In the first place, she should not be writing notes in class."

Lynn: "She should be more careful about passing around information that isn't true."

NOTE: A major difference between a primary and an intermediate Class Meeting is that in the primary the teacher decides upon the punishment or consequences; usually no suggestions are given by classmates. In the intermediate grades, the teacher serves more as a facilitator guiding the students to decide upon consequences. Also, the teacher encourages classmates to offer constructive tips to the erring student.

Responsibilities of the teacher

- Ask students' opinions, yet keep them on the topic.
- Avoid being judgmental.
- If a humiliating comment is made such as, "He is so dumb," ask other students what they think about the statement. Say, "Do you think there might be another reason for this behavior?"
- The teacher may stop the Class Meeting at any time to ask a question.
- Be open-minded and willing to let your students express themselves.
- After the initial Class Meeting, teacher input should diminish.
- Don't expect to be perfect. You'll make mistakes because social-problem solving is not easy.

Benefits to students: Class Meetings are important. Not only do they provide a natural time during the day to bring up problems, they also teach students to solve them. As an added bonus, your students will be learning to refine their thoughts and ideas, polish language skills and develop leadership potential.

In this chapter you have learned the importance of the Class Meeting in the intermediate HIP classroom. In the next chapter you will see how the ladder of discipline in the HIP room makes your teaching day easier.

10

Discipline Procedures

Nicole, a third grader, is every teacher's dream. She is quiet, cooperative, intelligent — in short, a constant delight. Josh who sits next to her in West Station is quite the opposite. He talks constantly, gets into fights and simply doesn't care how many points he loses for his station.

Unfortunately, some students in your classroom will refuse to cooperate in the room, in line, outside or anywhere. This is when more serious consequences are needed. An excellent way to approach this problem is by establishing a discipline ladder to keep behavior-problem students from disrupting your HIP room. Explain to your students that the ladder consists of a number of consequences for breaking classroom and school rules. Each ascending "step" carries more weight and is necessary in a room filled with students.

WALKING THE PERIMETER

Walking the Perimeter is a good way to get students to shape up. This is a device which uses the P.E. period as a time to discipline misbehaving students who will not respond to classroom peer pressure.

Example: Russ has been bugging people all week and repeatedly losing points for his station. His favorite subject is physical education, and he loves to play soccer. On a particularly bad day, warn Russ by putting his name on the chalkboard. Tell him that if he breaks another rule, he *chooses* to put himself on the Perimeter during P.E.

If he does break another classroom rule, write the word "Perimeter" after his name and tell him he must walk the Perimeter today while his classmates play soccer.

"Perimeter" is a line of your choosing on the blacktop or an imaginary line between two trees or any two points you designate as the "Perimeter Line" for your students. If you have a blacktop, pick a long painted line paralleling the area where your students will be playing. Since Russ loves to play soccer, you'll make much more impact disciplinewise if the class plays soccer while he walks the Perimeter. No matter where you are playing, you must be able to see Russ walking the line.

Before students start to walk the Perimeter, remind them that they must not run, play, fool around or stop to rest. Let them know that if they do, they are *choosing* to walk the Perimeter the next day and the next, if necessary. Emphasize that this is the student's responsibility; you will not issue any reminders.

While your class is playing, you must stay aware of Russ and what he is doing, but you should not speak to him. Once you return to the classroom, ask him to come up and erase his own name off the board if he behaved properly. Then have the class do a Three-Clap. If he did not behave as desired, identify the misbehavior. For example, you might say, "Russ, I saw you playing with a tennis ball while you were walking the Perimeter today. You *chose* to walk the Perimeter again tomorrow.

You should not have many students walking the Perimeter as most of them will obey class rules in order to participate in P.E.

Intermediate Discipline

Physcial education period is of vital importance to most intermediate students. Walking the Perimeter can be used, but often just placing older students against a wall or fence so they can observe the rest of the class involved in an activity is sufficient.

If the problem is minor, placing a student "out of circulation" for fifteen minutes is enough time for the boy or girl to get the message. If not, missing an entire period of physical education can make a radical difference in behavior. At the same time, others observing the student are also seeing what could happen to them.

HIP TIP: Never allow other students to taunt, tease or ridicule a student being punished. The punishment is simply being left out of an activity.

For additional ideas on limit setting, see page 129 in Teacher Resources.

The Next Step: SOS

Not only must you be concerned with the misbehaving students in your classroom, but you must also be sensitive to each station's overall morale. Stations with several misbehaving students can quickly become discouraged over constant loss of points. They may fear never having the opportunity to take part in the Monday Jobs distribution or to become class president.

To address this problem, you must speak to the misbehaving student, saying, "If you *choose* to continue losing points for your station, you will become an 'SOS' which stands for 'student-out-of-station.'" Explain to the class that if any student loses three points during the week, he or she will be placed out-of-station.

Explain that any student who *chooses* to lose three points for the station will have his or her name placed on the board with "SOS" beside it. Then tell the class that any SOS student will be last in line for recess, lunch and P.E. even if their station is ahead and goes out first. The SOS student must remain until you are ready to leave the room.

After the class has filed outside for recess, for example, take your time getting your things together before leaving. This will further emphasize the point that good behavior pays off and poor behavior does not.

HIP TIP: Keep in mind that an SOS student remains in his or her seat in the station. During lessons, the student can be called upon for answers to questions concerning the lesson. However, at all other times SOS students are to be ignored. They need to feel the "aloneness" of not being part of the group. This will be a great incentive for them to shape up immediately.

While discussing SOS consequences, tell the class that SOS students must earn five points to get back into their station. Only then, may they erase their name from the chalkboard and again become part of the station with all the rights and privileges of other students.

Also, emphasize that getting back into the station might take time. For example, Randy was SOS before early recess one morning, but he soon earned a point for his station and then another. The extra points were noted in the total for North Station where he was seated, as well as next to his own name on the chalkboard. By afternoon recess he had earned a third point for his station, but he got into trouble with another student and lost a point. This point was not removed from his station's total but it was noted after his name. He had to work hard the remainder of the day to earn back the lost point and the additional two so he could return to his station

If SOS doesn't work

Unfortunately, some students in your class will continue to engage in hurtful actions against others no matter how many times they walk the Perimeter or are placed on SOS. You should keep an anecdotal record on these students because it is sometimes necessary to go outside the classroom for help. Talk it over with the principal and the parents. If a school counselor is available, arrange a meeting to discuss the problem. It is important that you have records to back up your complaints or you'll look and feel very foolish if you can't substantiate your claims.

At times, after digging deeper into the issue, you will find major changes or ongoing problems in the home which upset the student and carry over into the classroom. Putting such students on behavior contracts can work well if the parents will cooperate with you. If they refuse, you as teacher, and peer pressure from the stations can still have an influence upon the particular student.

To set up daily contracts, meet with both student and parents, if possible, and discuss the need for the contract and exactly what it is. Either you or the student takes a three-by-five card and writes the student's name and the date at the top of the card. To make the whole process easier, make a month's supply of cards at once. Give the student a card at the end of each day. By prearrangement with the parents, your signature with a happy face means a good day. Your signature with a huge "X" means a bad day.

HIP TIP: Hide the cards in a safe place. I've had problem students take them from my desk, make a happy face and dash home.

Encourage parents to discover something the child really wants and to tell the student how many cards equal the promised gift. One of my students loved to ride his mini-bike on weekends. He would shape up in a hurry in order to get five good cards so he could ride. If I noticed him getting ready to hit someone, I'd pantomime a big "X" in the air and he would stop at once. I never had to say a word.

Keeping in close touch with the home is important so students know that what goes on at school is not a separate part of their lives. The home influence, along with yours, can frequently bring about an amazing change in a child's behavior.

HIP TIP: With many of your students coming from other countries, you'll discover that a number of parents cannot speak English. Some students take advantage of this when you seek to get them to behave. However, do not let this interfere with your discipline program. Ask around and you can almost be sure that an older brother or sister in junior high or high school speaks English. Ask them to bring the parents to school and have the student interpret for you. Be sure the misbehaving student also sits in on the conference. For more information on how to work with students and parents from other countries, see page 129 in Teacher Resources.

As behavior changes for the better take place with a problem student, suggest positive ways for the class to acknowledge them. "Three-Claps" for getting through the day without having to walk the Perimeter or the class voting to have the student lead the class over to the library instead of the president, tells problem students loud and clear that good behavior *PAYS OFF*.

OTHER METHODS FOR DEALING WITH BEHAVIOR PROBLEMS

Sending students to the office: Sending a misbehaving student to the office is seldom a solution to the problem because the office often becomes an "Entertainment Center" for the problem child. He or she might hear an outraged parent yelling at the principal, watch the PTA president make popcorn for the Friday sale or observe two kindergartners playing "hide and seek" under the detention bench.

Suspension: At one time even the threat of suspension was enough to make an erring student sit up and take notice. Not so today. With so many parents working, or others refusing to come to school and pick up their misbehaving students, this method is not as effective as it once was.

However, if you are in a situation where you've tried every other method to get the student to behave, then talk with your principal and consider suspension. Alert the parents ahead of time of your intent to suspend this child for his or her next rule infraction.

HIP TIP: Be sure you keep good anecdotal notes on your students with behavior problems. This can be done on a small card kept in your desk. Note date and time and a few brief words about what happened. You'll need this as backup should the parents question your decision to suspend.

In-house suspension: If you have a place in your classroom that is away from others where the student can sit quietly and work, this type of suspension has proven effective. However, many rooms are too overcrowded to have a suitable place to isolate a misbehaving student.

Teacher-to-teacher suspension: This is one of the best methods to use. Early in the year plan with another teacher to exchange misbehaving students when necessary. You should each have a spare desk in the back of your room and call each other when a misbehaving student is to leave one room for the other. The student is to bring work to do, will be given no privileges, and is ignored at all times. Should more misbehavior occur, add time to the suspension period.

After-school suspension: This can be a very effective method to get the message across to students that they must change their ways. If a group of teachers can work out a plan for rotating supervision, this is an outstanding plan. Not only do you force the student to stay after school, but you also require that he or she bring homework to do before being allowed to leave.

Again, there are negatives. Students who ride school busses often cannot stay after school. Or you may not find enough teachers willing to cooperate to keep a detention schedule going.

IMPORTANT: Whenever you keep a child after school, be sure to alert the parents first. It can create a major crisis when parents don't know the whereabouts of their children.

In this chapter you've learned the importance of a discipline ladder in the HIP classroom. In the next chapter you'll discover what an important part the P.E. program plays in the HIP classroom.

11

Kicking Toward Success

Whether they are six or sixteen, if you ask students their favorite subject, most will overwhelmingly say, "P.E." Teachers who tap into their students' enthusiasm for physical education activities can create an even more successful classroom.

In the HIP system, P.E. plays a vital part in the daily program. It can help students learn to cooperate with one another, with the teacher and with the umpire or any person making the decisions on plays. Students soon learn they are not always right and must abide by the rules of the game. They learn that both P.E. and life are a series of "give and take" experiences. Depending upon your class and your school's daily schedule, you can adjust the P.E. program to fit your students' needs.

Before school opens in September, have the year's plan in mind for your physical education program so you can direct your class in working out a cooperative schedule for the months ahead. If you don't plan, your students' eagerness for a specific game might lock you into one activity for the whole school year. This is not necessarily wrong but if you want to encourage your class to explore a variety of activities, make this clear at the beginning.

You may wish to have your class spend the first ten minutes of each physical education period doing exercises, for example. Then you may want to encourage your students to play soccer one week, kickball the next and another sport after that. For an outstanding physical education resource, see page 130 in Teacher Resources.

SELECTING TEAM CAPTAINS IN PRIMARY GRADES

Here is how to begin the P.E. program with your class: After the Monday Job Meeting, and prior to your scheduled P.E. period, arrange a few minutes to select captains and team members.

The two captains for the week will be chosen from the station with the most points.

Frequently everyone wants to be a captain and anyone in the winning station may be nominated for the position, even someone already elected to another job. This means you could have ten students who wish to be captains and even the president and vice president can be selected. Follow the same procedure for captain nominations as you do for job holders in Chapter 6.

After a student is nominated to be a captain, ask whom he or she would like to have as co-captain. The student can select anyone in the classroom, and usually there will be plenty of eager classmates from which to choose.

Record the nominations for team, captain and co-captain, and conduct the election just as you did for the jobs. Have students stand, then go through the entire list. The two pairs of students with the most votes become captains and co-captains for the week. Have captains select their teams in any manner you feel would be best, perhaps varying the process from week to week. Also, captains should alternate sexes as they pick their teams.

After the teams are selected, they huddle with their captains to decide upon team names. At the first of the year, you might want to help the class pick out team names. *Example:* Suggest the first week that they choose a two-word title with the first being a color and the second an animal. Students become creative in coming up with names such as Pink Alligators, Purple Elephants and Silver Unicorns. The second week suggest they pick names from the science lesson. For instance, if the class will be studying beetles, they might come up with interesting names such as Creepy Beetles, Monster Beetles or Demon Beetles.

Put both team names on the board and record the ongoing total of runs or points for each day's activity.

The captains serve for one week. New captains, teams and names are chosen the following Monday. This gives more students the opportunity to serve as captains and to develop leadership qualities in the classroom.

HIP TIP: Some captains are more popular than others and tend to be chosen over and over. If this happens and you get grumbling from other students, consider holding a Class Meeting to discuss the problem. See Chapters 8 and 9. When I did this, the class voted that Angie, who had been a captain four weeks out of six, should not be a captain again for one month. Angie agreed that this was fair.

Games such as kickball or baseball start Monday and end on Friday. Keep track of which team is up first and which student leads off each day. At the end of a game, indicate on your sheet the student who will go up first the following day. That way everyone gets a turn in order and no one is left out.

HIP TIP: Some students are timid or awkward in athletics. Encourage the more competent players in your class to work with less talented classmates on particular skills during recess and lunch breaks. Peer tutoring can achieve fantastic results with shy students, resulting in the buildup of self-esteem and physical skill for both the student and peer teacher.

PHYSICAL EDUCATION IN THE INTERMEDIATE GRADES

When using the committee approach to the physical education program, it is up to the selected committee to work out the games for the month.

At the same time, it is vital that the teacher is always aware of the planning going on within the various committees. Arrange for a time before or after school or during lunch to meet with the various committees each week. This way you'll know what to expect and the students will be aware that certain rules and procedures must be followed.

Here are some activities which intermediate students enjoy playing.

1. Basketball
2. Volleyball
3. Softball
4. Soccer
5. Football

It is important that students spend five to ten minutes doing warm-up activities such as stretching before beginning any activity. This warm-up period should be led by the physical education committee.

For more information on warm-ups, endurance and arm/leg/abdominal strength activities, see page 130 in Teacher Resources.

In this chapter you have learned about the importance of the physical education program in a HIP classroom. Remember, too, that P.E. time can be effectively used to enforce classroom discipline.

In the next chapter you'll discover ways to provide your students a scheduled time to talk, build their self-esteem and develop their oral skills.

12

Station Breaks

TELLING TIME!

NEWS!

SHARING!

*T*he majority of children love to talk. They talk to themselves, they talk to their pets, they talk to each other.

The HIP system takes advantage of this natural ability by providing specific times each day for oral expression in the classroom. These vocal activities, led by the class president, provide a time for students to develop leadership skills, speaking competency and the overcoming of fears when talking to a group.

HIP teachers are constantly seeking ways to demonstrate democracy in action. Through the use of "Telling the News," "Tell Time" or "Sharing," depending upon grade level, each student's presentation is important whether it's a current event, something heard on television or showing off a new family pet.

HIP TIP: As more and more of our students come to us from foreign countries, we need to provide them with opportunities to listen to others speak so they can learn our language. It is also wise to encourage our limited-English students to take part in Tell Time, Telling the News and Sharing. Often their bringing in a picture or memento from their home country gives a natural way for them to open up to us.

Here are explanations for the oral activities found in HIP classrooms:

PRIMARY — TELLING THE NEWS

In many schools, children in kindergarten and first grade often bring a special toy to school, tell where they got the toy, how much it costs (if known) and where they keep it in their home. The term most commonly used for this activity is "Show and Tell."

In HIP rooms the term is "Telling the News." This expression encompasses the Show and Tell idea but it goes beyond, because students in HIP rooms are urged to study newspapers, books and magazines.

Those who take the time to read an interesting article in the paper and present it to the class, for example, earn extra points for their station. This generates interest in sharing current events with the class, is more educational than showing off a new toy and is more considerate to those children for whom toys are few and far between.

PRIMARY — TELL TIME

"Tell Time" is simply telling about a subject which interests the child or would teach the other students something of interest. *Example:* A student might tell about visiting a grandfather who lives in the California mountains. He or she might tell about hunting for gold with the grandfather. The student would describe the cold water in the stream, how to hold the gold pan and tell about any nuggets found.

Another student might choose to talk about going to the Statue of Liberty, while someone else might talk about "how scared I was when my little sister swallowed too many aspirin tablets and we had to rush her to the hospital in the middle of the night."

Tell Time serves as a vehicle for students to vent their feelings. *Example:* Robert requested that the teacher ring the bell for Tell Time. Since the class was behind in completing a math assignment, the teacher hesitated. After two more urgent requests from Robert, the teacher rang the bell. Soon it became apparent why Robert needed Tell Time just then. His Air Force father had been transferred to Japan. Robert explained where his father was stationed (a student held the world globe) and he told how much he missed his father and how long it would be until the rest of the family could join him in Japan.

PREPARING STUDENTS FOR TELLING THE NEWS AND TELL TIME

In the HIP classroom in September, it is important to prepare students for Telling the News and Tell Time. Some students shy away from getting up in front of classmates. This is especially true for new students. These fears need to be recognized.

HIP TIP: During the first week of the new school year, lead the class in an oral discussion by asking questions such as: "Where did you go this summer?" or, "What is your favorite food?" or "Tell us about your pet." As you go from student to student, assure them that they can say "pass" and the next time they can share with the group.

The second week, begin to call upon those who wish to talk. Say, "You may stand at your seat to talk or you may come up and stand by the Chairman-of-the-Board table." To build excitement say, "Now Randy in South Station will bring us a special report." Or, "Carmen has a newsflash for all of us from North Station." Use terms like, "special bulletin, in-depth report, and flash." Since students watch so much television, they will relate to these terms at once.

During the first month of school, you are the model for conducting Telling the News and Tell Time. The way you conduct the meeting is the way the future president will direct the meetings from October onward.

THE PRESIDENT PRESIDES

After the presidential election in early October, the president will conduct Telling the News and Tell Time while sitting in the teacher's chair at the Chairman-of-the-Board table. The bailiff sits in a chair near the HIP chart. During Telling the News and Tell Time, the bailiff, under the teacher's direction, removes or adds points to specific stations if necessary.

The president begins with the station having the most points. *Example:* South Station is in the lead. The president asks all students in South Station who brought something to share to raise their hands. He or she then selects a student to come to the front of the room.

After the student makes the presentation, the president should be prepared to lead a discussion. Here are sample questions: "Who gave you the old coin?" "How much is it worth?" Or, "Could any of you bring a coin book so we can look it up?" Then the discussion is opened to the class members. Frequently, the answers to students' questions will clarify a too-short presentation given by a nervous, shy student.

After all students in South Station who wish to share have had a turn, the president turns to the station with the next-most points and then to the last station, giving all who want an opportunity to share. Some days half the class might share, while on other days only five or six might come prepared. The entire activity should not take over fifteen minutes. If the meeting tends to lag, urge students to shorten their presentations to a few sentences.

During Telling the News, you should be able to walk quietly back to the parent table where you can relax while the class president conducts the meeting — but this is not always possible. Sometimes, depending upon the makeup of your class, you may need to sit in the vacant president's chair in his or her station. In this way you take an active part in Telling the News if you find students fail to cooperate with the class president. Classes can be very different and you must decide what works best for you with each one.

PRIMARY PARADE

At the end of Telling the News, the president announces, "Parade." He or she stands near the Chairman-of-the-Board table and waits for all students who participated in Telling the News to line up. Then, at the direction of the teacher, the president can lead the parade, or ask the bailiff to lead.

The parade is simply a HIP classroom activity which gives students the opportunity to show at close range what they brought to school. They can also answer individual questions from students as they pass in front of their desks. HIP students may choose to stay at their desks but they are urged to move to the front of the "U" and stand quietly while the parade passes in front of them. Only students who brought items for Telling the News will be in the parade. Afterward all large items should be placed on the window counter or some other designated area, and small items should go inside students' desks.

ADDITIONAL PARADE IDEAS

The parade need not be limited to a daily Telling the News. When a parent comes to school to show off a student's turtle, for instance, ask the president to stand at the front of the room and lead a special parade which might only include the student, the turtle and the president as leader.

When other classes come to your room to exhibit their art work, for example, ask the bailiff or president to lead a parade of the visiting students.

The teacher signals when the parade is over by ringing a bell, making a prearranged arm motion, or sounding a note on the piano. Students must return immediately to their desks or lose points.

Students also need to know that if they play during the day with toys brought for Telling the News, they are *choosing* to have points removed from their station.

HIP TIP: Make a firm rule at the beginning of the year that all Telling-the-News items must go home at the end of each day. The first few weeks, make such an announcement just prior to dismissal to help remind the class, but don't continue these daily reminders. Make it the students' responsibility. If students continually forget to take Telling-the-News items home, take points off their station.

SHARING

In the intermediate grades, "Sharing" is used as a way for older students to share a favorite hobby with fellow students, show off a skirt made during vacation or present a current event to the class.

In the HIP intermediate classroom, Sharing means students talk about, for example, a recent trip to the ocean, a personal happening, or add some additional information about a previous science lesson on geology. The student may have taken the time to look up the definitions for obsidian, granite and limestone, or brought specimens from a rock collection.

When students do this extra work, their station should be awarded extra points, with the number reflecting the amount of work involved in researching and bringing the report to the class.

Sharing can also be a time for venting feelings for the student. *Example:* talking about the death of a grandparent, an upcoming move or being elected leader of a Cub Scout den.

HIP TIP: At the beginning of the year, lay the ground rules for newspaper, television and magazine reports. Let students know you will not accept any reports on grisly murders, auto crashes or bombings. Students tend to get emotionally caught up in the gory details and pictures of such stories and miss the facts. The following day, someone is bound to bring in an even more horrible story for an "I-can-top-that."

Whether teaching in the primary or intermediate grades, encourage students to bring in news which would serve as a learning experience for the entire class. Also, when a student talks on a subject where "big" words are used, suggest that if a student brings back a definition of the word the next day, a certain number of points can be earned for the station. If the reporting student has already made the effort to know the definition of the word, the points should be added to his or her station then. Use this technique of reporting as a tool for expanding the class's knowledge on a variety of subjects.

In this chapter you've learned how Telling the News, Tell Time and Sharing are special ways you can use a student's zeal for talking as a learning experience for all students in the classroom. You've also seen that Telling the News, Tell Time and Sharing are ways of building self-confidence, self-esteem and good oral-expression skills in students.

In the next chapter you will discover how Telling the News, Tell Time and Sharing give you a welcome rest from your non-stop day.

13

Time Out

Surveys taken in classrooms indicate teachers make 500 decisions each hour, second only in number to air traffic controllers. No wonder harried, hassled and hurried teachers look forward to weekends so they can enroll in stress-reducing workshops.

But you need not wait until the weekend for a change of pace. In the HIP classroom, all you need to do is schedule a brief oasis of restful calm in your busy, busy day.

The HIP room is set up so that the class president, after watching your example at the beginning of the school year, is well prepared to take over Telling the News, Tell Time or Sharing.

While the president does this, the bailiff sits at the Honor Point chart and adds or removes points. This makes HIP students aware that even when you are not in front of the room, the built-in disciplinary plan continues. The structure of the system provides you with your own personal "Time Out."

SCHEDULED SERENITY

Keep Telling the News or Sharing as a regularly scheduled part of your lesson plan with the president taking over for you.

Tell Time, on the other hand, should be saved for the inevitable interruptions which arrive. For example if the principal needs to talk to you for a few minutes, ring the bell or snap your fingers and ask the students to clear their desks. Then say, "President, please conduct Tell Time." This will give you time to devote all your attention to the principal, a parent or other unexpected visitors.

CONSECUTIVE NUMBERS — PRIMARY GRADES

Students in the early primary grades frequently have a problem saying and writing numbers — even from one to one hundred. Many can write a few in correct sequence but often they get mixed up when they reach numbers like "39" and cannot recall what comes next. They continually come to the teacher and ask, "What comes after 59, 69 or 79?"

One method for teaching individual students to count in order is to put them at a large table and give them a pencil, one hundred pennies and many small pieces of paper. Have them set a penny on a piece of paper and mark the slip "1." They should continue to place pennies and number the slips in order from one to one hundred. This works well with one student but is too difficult to arrange for a number of pupils needing extra help at the same time.

In the HIP classroom, students in the primary segment practice their numbers by writing from one onward as far as they can go, sometimes up into the thousands. Here is how to arrange this activity:

At the beginning of the year, plan an art activity where each pupil makes a "Number Book." Provide each student with a manila folder. Using colored chalk on the chalkboard, design a number book for them as a model. The title can be "My Number Book" or "My Number Folder."

Hold a class discussion about the various ways students can decorate them. By suggesting a prize or extra HIP points for the top three winners, you can usually ensure some spectacular artwork.

After the covers are finished, pass out five sheets of regular lined newsprint to each student. Have them fold the paper lengthwise in half and then again, making four columns. Ask them to put their names on each sheet and number the pages in order. Staple the pages to the inside of the folders.

Instruct the students to begin writing number "1" and then "2" and on down the column. I used the overhead the first couple of days and wrote along with the class so I knew they were following directions and doing the numbers correctly.

The object is to see how far students can write their numbers in correct order. Suggest when they are not sure of the next number, they can refer to the page numbers in a dictionary or an old, large telephone book which you can provide in the classroom.

Students love competition and you can spark their interest by having a drawing every Monday. The three highest numbers drawn will be the students getting the prizes that week. It's not unusual to hear a student tell a neighbor, "I'm up to 1,800 now and I'm going to get to 2,000 by next week."

Soon after beginning this project, check to find at least one outstanding "consecutive-number" student in each station to act as a helper. When visitors step into the room to talk to you, you can ask the class to take out their Number Books. Then ask the helpers in each station to walk around and assist those having problems. This is another way of providing you with a "Time-Out" break, when needed.

MULTIPLICATION FACTS — INTERMEDIATE

One of the most difficult concepts to teach in math is division. It becomes even more of a problem because students refuse to learn their multiplication facts.

HIP TIP: A study indicates that students must write, see or hear a math fact, spelling word or vocabulary word *twenty-six times* before it is permanently imprinted in the brain. As teachers we must find ways to have students do their number facts over and over without burning them out.

One way of making this into a game in the intermediate classroom is to have your students keep a "Multiplication Folder" in their desk at all times. Not only must they keep it in the desk, but also you'll need to provide them with an incentive to use it on a daily basis.

HINT: Do not allow folders to go home. If you do, students may cheat by writing many, many facts to become eligible for the prize on Monday mornings. Also, folders often do not come back or may have pages torn out so you cannot have a correct count on the number of facts written.

MULTIPLICATION FOLDER — INTERMEDIATE

During the first week of school when your students are settling down, pass out a manila folder to each student. On the chalkboard or overhead projector draw the folder and print the words "Multiplication Folder." Using colored chalk, draw an interesting design using multiplication and division problems in a unique manner. See example.

Then show the students how you want them to fold 8 1/2" x 11" lined newsprint into four long columns. See example on the next page.

Explain that before they begin the project, they will have an art period to draw and color their most creative cover designs. Tell them that the folders will be placed on the chalkboard trays the next day to be voted upon by fellow

students. Ask them not to put their names on the front until after the voting is completed. Instead, identify them by writing numbers on the chalkboard above each folder. On a slip of paper, students list the three numbers which indicate their favorite folders. Their creators are then each given a prize for their artwork.

After the voting, your students will staple seven pages of lined newsprint folded into columns, into their folders. They are to number down each column starting with "1" and continue to the end of the page and on to the next. This is important when it is time to determine the student with the most multiplication facts for the prize. See illustration.

NOTE: Have one person in each station designated to review the facts to be sure they are accurate before any prizes are given.

HIP TIP: Before beginning this project, give your students a quickie multiplication fact test. For example, ask them to write their multiplication facts from seven times zero to seven times twelve. Then ask them to write three other sets of facts such as fives, nines and twelves. After looking over this test, you'll know your students' weak areas.

The day after the quickie multiplication facts test, tell your students to take out their Multiplication Folders. As you model the lesson on the overhead projector, they will write along with you. Explain that many of them did not know their sevens (they will all loudly deny this) and today they will write their sevens facts five times in their folders. They will begin at the top of the first column and write in order to the bottom and then go to the next column.

From that time onward when they have free time in the classroom, they are to take out their folders and write as many of the multiplication facts as they can.

MONDAY PRIZE

Each Monday have a drawing to keep the interest going. Have all of your students take out their folders. Then provide them with a slip of paper on which they write their name and the number of facts they have written.

HINT: Instead of handing in a slip, many will quickly start writing like mad to make up for lost time. Explain this is not the time to write facts and refuse to let them continue this practice. It takes up valuable time in the classroom.

Ask the vice president to pass a basket around to collect the folded slips of paper. The vice president takes the basket to the Chairman-of-the-Board table and picks out three slips. All three students receive a prize but the student with the highest number of the three gets a double prize. Actually, it's really not having the most multiplication facts but rather the luck of the draw for the winners. Since students enjoy watching the slips being drawn out of the basket, they can hardly wait to see if they might be a winner. This keeps their enthusiasm going.

SUGGESTIONS FOR PRIZES

1. The winning students may go to the cafeteria five minutes early for lunch. Be sure to let the cafeteria manager know you are doing this.
2. Winners may spend an extra ten minutes in the computer lab. Again, clear this first with the computer lab teacher.
3. A winning student may be president for one day.
4. You may hand out coupons for free food at a local fast-food store.
5. Have a bag filled with a variety of "prizes" you've collected, and let each winner reach in and pick one, sight unseen.

HINT: In some classes it might be necessary to look at folders to be sure students are being honest about how many facts they have written.

HIP TIP: Do not let students write incorrect facts. This will only slow down the process of learning. Instead, have them open their math books to the multiplication fact chart, or provide students with small charts with their names on them. Insist students keep them inside their math books at all times. See Teacher Resources page 130 for sample multiplication facts folder which can be copied and laminated to keep it neat and clean.

STUDENT JOURNALS: A TOTAL LANGUAGE ACTIVITY

Another idea which students enjoy on a daily basis, particularly in the intermediate grades, is a journal. Students can bring inexpensive notebooks from home or they may cut good, lined paper in half. They can make front and back covers from construction paper to form the booklet. Again, have your students spend an art period designing a cover for the journal. Use competition, an art grade or HIP points as an incentive to do good work.

For a Total Language activity, each day have your students write a page about something happening in the room, a new pet at home or something special going on in their lives. This gives them practice in creative writing and, since the teacher will not be grading this activity, it becomes even more enjoyable. Again, when the teacher needs a "Time Out," students can take out their journals. During Sharing, some students may wish to show a page or two describing something special in their lives. They should be encouraged to do this. For more information on journal writing see page 130 in Teacher Resources.

PREP TIME

In many elementary classrooms now, the librarian or prep teachers specializing in art or music will take your class for a period once or twice a week to give you time to prepare your lesson plans or other necessary work.

Sometimes the prep teachers take your class to another area, leaving you free to work in peace. In most cases, however, the prep teacher brings all materials on a cart and teaches in your classroom. This means you must either stay in the back of the room or go to the faculty lounge.

By all means, go to another room. If you stay in the classroom, you'll get caught up in solving behavior problems as they develop. Even if you forget something, do not go back to the classroom. You can be sure several students will be waiting to report or tattle on others and expect you to use your precious time to settle the problem. The room is now being run by the prep teacher and she or he should settle all problems.

HIP TIP: If your district does not have prep time each week for teachers, fight for it. Junior high and high school teachers have had it for years. Fifteen years ago an elementary teacher joined with three other teachers and formed a group to work on getting her district to include a prep period twice a week for all elementary teachers. After months of meetings, the board finally accepted the recommendation. Many teachers today are grateful for the time and effort of a few teachers who brought this about.

TIPS FOR TIME OUT

Now that you have several opportunities each day to take a change of pace, here are some dos and don'ts:

DON'T

- Reach for a stack of uncorrected papers while the class president is conducting Telling the News, Tell Time or Sharing. Instead, give yourself the luxury of doing absolutely nothing during these few precious minutes. You owe it to yourself and to your students to relax.
- Rush to your desk and grab your class register and feverishly complete the monthly tabulation due in the office later in the day. Rather, enjoy "the quiet now" and plan to complete the register when the students are gone for the day.
- Dash up to the Chairman-of-the-Board table and reach for your Lesson Plan book in hopes of getting a head start on writing lesson plans for the following week. Again, relax, enjoy! Even if you cannot be "Queen or King for a Day," you can be for ten whole minutes!

DO

- Arrange a special place in the back of the room where you can rest during these time outs. Settle in the most comfortable chair at the table set aside for parents and unwind while the president presides over Telling the News or Sharing.

- Remember that your only need for action comes if someone in a station is making a real disturbance. Then all you need say is, "Bailiff, (or Teacher Assistant), take five points away from South Station. Someone there is looking around and not paying attention." This is usually all that is needed to get the attention of all the stations and alerts potential problem makers to stop what they are doing.
- Make a conscious decision to relax physically. If you have never taken a course in relaxation, consider getting one of the many books or tapes available to learn relaxation techniques. With practice, you can notice a real difference in only three or four minutes.

For additional information on stress-reducing books and tapes, see page 131 in Teacher Resources.

In this chapter you have discovered how important it is to nourish your mental, emotional and physical well-being and how you can make the time to do this.

In the next chapter you'll discover how to motivate your students to do their best work in the HIP classroom.

14

Reaching for the Stars

Ten-year-old Becky has an album with over a hundred stickers she earned memorizing the times tables. She loves to show it off at family gatherings.

Mike, a fourth grader, is a Cub Scout. He has worked hard all year to earn his Bear patch which he proudly wears on his uniform.

Laura, a fifth grader, is determined to get five "A's" on her report card. If she does, her grandmother will buy her a cassette tape player and five of her favorite tapes.

The majority of children love to compete for awards, to work toward goals and be winners. Teachers can use this natural drive to encourage students to do their best in school through the simple device of the star card to reward daily achievers.

HIP TIP: Some students refuse to do their best and do not try to achieve. For these few, you must come up with alternative methods to encourage them to do their best work. Positive praise for a job well done, a Three-Clap or snapping of fingers by the class when a project is completed and happy notes sent home can often make a difference in the attitudes of reluctant learners.

Star cards, when used in the HIP classroom, encourage students to do their best work. While stations are rewarded with HIP points, students are rewarded with stars for outstanding personal work. Individual creativity, neatness and correct work translate into stars on each student's card.

THE STAR CARD SYSTEM

Provide each student in the class with a 5 x 7" card in an unusual color such as pink, blue or yellow. (Do not use white cards as they are more available and some ingenious student will try to duplicate them.) Have each student put his or her name on the card in the top right corner. On the left have them write, "Star Card." To further cut down on counterfeit cards, use pens or pencils in special colors.

HIP TIP: Take a box used for manila folders or a shoe box and cover the box and lid with paper such as a vivid green or blue. Then stick both silver and gold stars all over the top and sides of the box. If you wish to be more dramatic, write "Star Box" with white glue on the side of the box, then sprinkle the glue with glitter! Students lift the lid and place their cards inside when they have collected twenty stars and they will find the box irresistible.

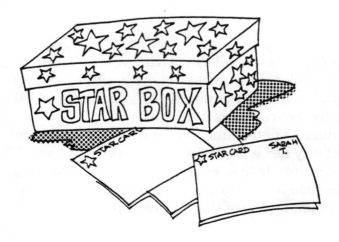

PRIMARY—MAKING THE STAR SYSTEM WORK

At the beginning of the year tell the class that they will be responsible for keeping their cards in their desks. Explain that the only time the cards should be out is for reading, math, the Friday spelling test and, at your instructions, during certain language periods.

Tell the students you will come by during reading and math to check their daily work. If they have an "A" paper, you will draw a star on their card.

The stars are very useful when students write sentences or paragraphs in language. You can determine, depending upon the grade, how many stars should be given for various levels of work. (Students need to know that a sentence such as, "The boy runs," lacks "star quality.")

Stars should also be used for special occasions when a subject such as "Fire Prevention in the Forest," "Fishing on the Green River," or "The Day My Cat Died" has been assigned. Students can also earn stars by writing thank-you notes to a classroom guest speaker, a mother who dropped by with cupcakes or the custodian who fixed the lights in the classroom.

PRIMARY—OTHER WAYS FOR USING STAR CARDS

Small-group stars: Especially if your class is on the early-late reading program, the cards can help to promote good papers, along with independent work habits, when you are working with a small group.

"Early-late" means that half your class might come to school at 8:30 each morning while the remainder comes at 9:30. The early people go home first and the late readers stay an additional hour.

When you are working with a small reading group, it is essential that you are not interrupted by the rest of the students. If you have mothers who come to help or monitors who come in from the upper grades to supervise, they can also draw a star on the cards of students who have good work and behave well during the reading period.

Spelling stars: To encourage students to know their spelling words, give a star to each student who earns an "A" on Friday's spelling test. In addition, if you give bonus words such as Halloween, Christmas or the months of the year as part of the test, you may wish to give a star for each one spelled correctly.

Counting the stars: Students are not only in charge of keeping the cards but of calculating their own running tally. Tell them that when they get twenty stars, they will be eligible for a coupon to turn in for a prize. Direct them to put their card with the number "20" circled on the top into the star box. You

can double-check their counting later and issue a new card and a coupon. If a student forgets and ends up with twenty-five stars on a card, draw five stars on the new card.

STAR CARDS IN THE INTERMEDIATE CLASSROOM

Have students make Star Cards as described in the primary classroom. Explain that they may earn stars when they do outstanding research work and write a report for science, social studies or health. You may also wish to have them earn extra stars for outstanding work on spelling, math and reading tests.

Consider setting aside a bulletin-board area titled, "Star Achievers" to display outstanding projects. This will emphasize to your students the importance of doing good, clean and neat work of which they can be proud.

HIP TIP: When assigning a special science report, for example, explain that outstanding work will earn stars, and the paper will be posted along with the Star Card for all to see. The paper will serve as a model to show all students what you expect from them.

STAR PRIZES

Each teacher must decide how to award prizes. Here are a few suggestions which have worked well:

1. In some HIP classrooms, each filled Star Card is worth ten points for the student's station.
2. Hold an assembly once a month and have students bring their winning coupons. (Some schools call these Winner Assemblies.) At the end of the assembly, students turn in their winner coupons for a certificate donated by a fast-food chain in the area. Some convenience stores donate passes for winning students to play video games.
3. At the end of each month, some teachers choose to take the students with the most star cards for a burger or hot fudge sundae. See Chapter 15 for ways to raise funds for these "extras" in your classroom.

In this chapter you have learned the importance of challenging students to do their very best work. Star cards are one way of saying, "Well done. You are a winner!"

In Chapter 15 you'll discover ideas for time scheduling and fund raising.

15

Time and Money Management

One of the first teachers I told about the HIP program protested, "But I won't have time to *teach*!"

It might seem so at first, but I found I actually had *more* time available for productive teaching.

FLEXIBILITY

Although the basic format of the HIP classroom is highly structured, you'll need to remain flexible. Some days will pass smoothly; others will be so packed with just meeting subject deadlines that you'll glance at the clock and realize it's almost time for the class to go home. What then?

You'll learn that some days can become so hectic there is simply no time for Telling the News, Tell Time or Sharing. Assure students they may leave their sharing items at school until the next day when both activities will be conducted. But whenever possible, try to conduct your Tell Time or Sharing.

More disturbing is running out of time for your Class Meeting. Stop and explain that while there will not be time for a Class Meeting today, you will be sure to hold one tomorrow. Some students will be angry and will let you know how displeased they are. Remind these few, perhaps as they walk out the door, that sometimes it is impossible to fit everything into one day but they will have their day tomorrow.

For your own peace of mind, though, try to hold at least an abbreviated Class Meeting each day. Open by saying, "We only have time to hear an emergency type problem today." Often this is in the nature of a complaint such as, "Steve said he's going to beat me up on the way home from school. I'm afraid to leave." This should be addressed at once, not only for the safety of the fearful student but to alert Steve that everyone is onto him, so he had better watch out!

HIP TIP: Sometimes students will be afraid to go out for recess, lunch or to walk home because a student in another class threatened to "get them." Alert your fellow teachers at the beginning of the year that if their students make threats, you'll call their room and ask the student to come to your classroom during Class Meeting. At the same time, let the teachers know your students will be sent to their rooms if they threaten others. When the student arrives at your room, ask him or her to stand next to you at the front of the room and explain what happened. Most of the time the problem can be settled at once. This visit also alerts other students at school that if they misbehave, they must make an appearance in your classroom. A bonus is the sense of loyalty your own class will feel toward you. It gives them a feeling of added protection both inside and outside the classroom.

In the intermediate grades it is usually not as necessary to conduct daily Class Meetings but still aim to hold your meetings at least three times a week. While younger students often can't recall either the big or little things from one day to the next, intermediate students are older and can remember the important things. They can usually wait a day or two to discuss problems which they've written on the agenda. This sometimes even provides them with a natural cooling-off period. When there are one or two days between meetings, small problems may resolve themselves. On the other hand, some problems may escalate seriously, and those will have to be addressed as soon as possible.

KEEPING TRACK OF POINTS

It might appear that the pure mechanics of posting, adding and subtracting Honor Points will be cumbersome and time-consuming. However, you'll find that keeping track of points for big items brought to class each morning can be done in five minutes or less. During the rest of the day, stepping to the Honor chart takes only a moment. I sometimes simply note a "+1" or "-1" by the station in question and change the totals later.

HIP TIP: Remember when you are busy helping a student in the back of the room and notice a disturbance in a station, you need not leave the student you are helping. Instead, use your bailiff.

On mornings when I'm especially busy, I may not get to the Honor Point chart to change the totals for each station until just before recess or lunch. The same is true in the afternoon. I may not change them again till recess or just before the students go home. But the majority of the time, by student demand, I do keep the totals correct. This does not take long. Again, use the upgrading of points as a time to reinforce the learning of addition, subtraction, borrowing, carrying and multiplication of numbers.

Here is a plan which will save you much time keeping points:

At the beginning of the year, set aside a 24x24-inch portion of your chalkboard space for your HIP chart. This is enough for three stations. If you have more stations, add an extra eight inches of top-to-bottom space for each one. Place the chart on the far side of the board in an area where all the students can see it from their desks.

Now, using masking tape, make a permanent grid to keep track of points. See illustration.

Write station names in each of the three squares to the left. Use the second square for the running tally marks and the last column to total the tally as needed. This way you won't have to rewrite station names each Monday morning. Also, it gives the chart a neat and official look.

TEACHER TIME SAVERS

One of the great joys in the HIP program is not having to direct every activity every minute of the day. This means during Telling the News, Tell Time or Sharing I have my own private "Time Out" while the president conducts these activities. It is true that during some Time-Out periods, I must work on my register or talk with a parent. But the class moves forward very well without me in the front of the room. It is my time to breathe deeply, to regroup, to relax. For additional information on stress-reducing ideas, see page 131 in Teacher Resources, Chapter 13.

Another bonus is that I no longer have to keep misbehaving students after school. The system takes care of these problem students by subtracting points from their stations. This also means an immediate reprimand, as mentioned, from station mates for "doing this to us." And, if the peer pressure does not work, I use the Perimeter walk to remind the student to "settle down."

I think you too, will find that the HIP system will make you *feel* successful as you walk through each organized day.

MONEY MATTERS

Teachers vary widely in their views on spending their own money for the classroom. Some get by, by "making do." Others go all out, spending personal money year after year. For more ideas on how to save money in your classroom see page 131 in Teacher Resources.

In the HIP program, I did spend some personal funds in my classroom. But, I also found ways to help students raise money so we could do a few "extras" as pure pleasure or to pay for out-of-town field trips.

Money was spent to provide chocolate or candy bars each Friday for our reading tutors from the intermediate grades, for popcorn for special Friday movies and to take award-winning students to lunch once a month. I also purchased trinkets at a discount store and kept these in a grab bag as prizes for consecutive-numbers winners.

But you do not have to personally pay for these extras. Here are several teacher-tested ideas for raising money for your classroom projects:

Cupcake sales: Have a parent organize the sale. Give her or him the names of others you think might be willing to work. Ask each parent in your class to bake two dozen cupcakes. If some cannot, they should know that it will not in any way reflect on their child. Other mothers frequently are willing to bake additional cupcakes.

Caution: Some districts no longer allow homebaked foods in school for health reasons so make sure it's an approved activity before you start.

Advertise the sale for at least one week previous to the big day. Have your students design and paint colorful posters to place all around the school telling about the sale.

Newspaper recycling: Newspaper-recycling dealers are in the business of collecting LARGE amounts of papers. Take advantage of this. Ask a parent to head the campaign. Advertise widely in the community for at least one month prior to the Saturday collection date.

The typical paper dealer will provide you with a large lockable metal bin similar in size to the ones found on construction sites for waste materials. The bin is delivered by truck on a Friday to your school. On the designated Saturday have your students load up their wagons and their parents' cars and trucks with newspapers collected from their neighborhoods.

The papers are taken to the school site and the father in charge unlocks the metal bin and loads in the paper. The dealer will pick up the container on Monday, weigh it and pay your class. Prices vary from city to city so call your local recycling dealer for payment schedules.

Aluminum can collection: Another way to make extra money is to have your students collect aluminum cans. Keep a large plastic-lined garbage can in the back of your room. Encourage your students to rinse and smash the cans before bringing them into the classroom. Another possibility is to have a "smashing party" out on the playground as soon as the barrel is full of rinsed cans. You get the job done and kids love the action. It will also help you get the barrel filled up faster.

Caution: Before doing this, show your students how to "smash" the cans correctly. They need to stand away from others so a flying can does not hurt another student. Since recycling companies pay different amounts per pound from city to city, call your local dealer to get the exact price for your area. Ask a parent to be in charge of redeeming the cans when you have a good collection.

Saturday film shows: Showing a special film such as "Charlotte's Web," along with a cartoon in your multipurpose hall on a Saturday morning can bring in a large amount of money in a few hours.

Example: Outstanding films can be rented from Far West Films, Inc. in San Francisco. Call (415) 565-3000. Again, advertise widely for a week or two before the film showing. Enlist parents to be in charge of donating popcorn, Kool Aid and hot dogs for intermission treats. Not only do you charge admission, you also make money on the concessions. One teacher made over $300 doing this on a single Saturday morning.

These are certainly not the only ways of raising money for your classroom, but the suggestions may trigger some ideas of your own such as a class newspaper to sell to parents and other students.

Caution: I would discourage students from going door-to-door today selling candy, candles or other items. Too many neighborhoods are no longer safe for a child to go out selling unless accompanied by an adult.

For additional information on how to raise funds for your classroom, see page 131 in Teacher Resources.

CONCLUSION

Now that you've been introduced to the HIP system you may wish to try out the entire package or only parts of it. Only you know what will work best in your classroom. No management system is perfect for everyone.

For the most part, the HIP method of Classroom Management should work for you. However with the ever-increasing problems in our society, particularly in inner cities, there will be more and more children born to drug-or alcohol-addicted parents. In some years, you're sure to get one or more of these mentally and socially afflicted children. With such disruptive students, a few options might be counseling for them, advice from their family's social worker or workshops for you to possibly learn how to cope with the

situation. In some cases little or none of this help will be available. There may be years when most of what you do is only "tread water." Just remember if you're in this kind of a situation and you've exhausted all possible options for available help and the HIP program doesn't work as successfully for you as you had hoped, you can't feel guilty; it's not your fault.

If you do choose to use the HIP system, feel free to change it to fit your own particular classroom and students. Then enjoy a most successful school year.

In the next chapter you'll find reactions to the HIP program from students, teachers and parents.

16

Reactions to HIP

*T*he HIP method has been widely acclaimed by teachers, parents and students as an outstanding classroom management system. Students enjoy working in a HIP classroom where their votes count, their views can be expressed at Class Meetings and their stations win honors for achieving the most points.

PRIMARY STUDENTS' REACTIONS

Primary students look forward to the Job Meeting each Monday morning. They enjoy the responsibility of holding jobs in the classroom, seeing that the room is clean, books are in order and lights turned out. The first thing Monday morning, students often say, "Now don't forget to have the Job Meeting right away 'cause my station got the most points on Friday, right?"

Each month the HIP system also provides students the opportunity to become class president or vice president. They can hardly wait until the final day of the month to see if their station won. Explanation: The final Friday of the month is important to stations for two reasons: (1) If their station has the highest point count, they get the jobs for the following week. (2) In addition, since it is the end of the month, the station also gets to nominate the president and vice president for the following month. For this reason, students will work very hard the last few days of the month to try to get the honors.

My students and I were all enthusiastic about the start of the HIP program and its success from the beginning.

My primary parents were also happy with the procedures in the HIP classroom and often expressed their satisfaction with having their children in my room. "Mark is elated to have been elected class president," his father confided. "It's done wonders for his self- esteem." Erin's mother said, "Being class president has helped Erin to speak up and to talk more, which is something we had been trying to get her to do at home."

With one exception, the remaining parents who came into the room during the year to help or to visit were thrilled with the HIP classroom management system. One said to me, "My daughter is learning so much this year because she is in a room where there is order and discipline."

INTERMEDIATE STUDENTS' REACTIONS TO HIP

A fourth-grade teacher working in an inner-city school had a class filled with behavior problems. As a result, little teaching was going on. After taking a "How to Organize Your Classroom" workshop one Saturday, she asked her principal to allow her to go into her room on Sunday to prepare it for the HIP program.

At first her students were greatly distressed at having the room changed around. But by the end of the first week, they had settled down and seldom got into fights anymore. Several actually told her they thought that "HIP is great."

A split fifth- and sixth-grade class would not work together before the teacher tried the HIP system. The sixth graders wanted nothing to do with the fifth graders. They constantly expressed feelings of superiority toward them; this, in turn, created friction both in the classroom and out on the playground. Within three days after their first Class Meeting at which they addressed these problems and discussed the new rules and procedures, students were happily working together as a group.

HIP TIP: Be sure you don't overload any one station with behavior problems. When new students enter or old students leave, the personality of a station can change very quickly. Be alert to these changes and as soon as possible, see that all stations have a well-rounded balance of students.

PARENTS' REACTIONS TO THE HIP PROGRAM

My one exception to primary parents' early HIP enthusiasm was Mrs. Carson, the mother of eight-year-old Jessica. I was delighted when she came to see me before school opened and offered to help in the classroom.

One afternoon during the third week of school, she was grading papers in the back of the room when I rang the bell and announced, "Class Meeting." She continued to work quietly during the first ten minutes of the meeting, but then I noticed her hand waving in the air. After I finished with the station, I called on her. She said, "I think this meeting is ridiculous! These kids ought to know how to behave themselves. They don't need to be spending their time complaining about others calling them bad names and kicking them."

I briefly explained why we had the meeting, thanked her for her input and continued with the Class Meeting. Later, during a recess break, I took her to the Faculty Room and explained in more detail why we held Class Meetings. Since she had never worked in a classroom, she was not aware of the amount of time primary students spend tattling. I told her the meeting provided angry students with a place to let off steam, to resolve differences and to hear offenders say, "I'm sorry." Then I told her that after the built-in Class Meeting, we could spend the rest of the day doing schoolwork instead of having students constantly pouring out their difficulties with others to the teacher. After my explanation and seeing the program in action, Mrs. Carson also soon became an enthusiastic HIP supporter. She understood.

MY REACTIONS TO HIP

I was ready for HIP. I had just completed a difficult, demoralizing year with a class which was impossible to manage. I had pulled out my usual "bag of discipline tricks" gleaned over twenty years, but nothing worked.

That summer I spent my time saturating myself with HIP methods. Before school began I made notes on how to start the first day. These were typed on 5x7-inch cards which I attached to my Lesson Plans. I made similar notes for introducing Telling the News, Telling Time, the first Job Meeting and Class Meeting. I studied these notes until I fully understood each step and felt comfortable about introducing HIP to my students.

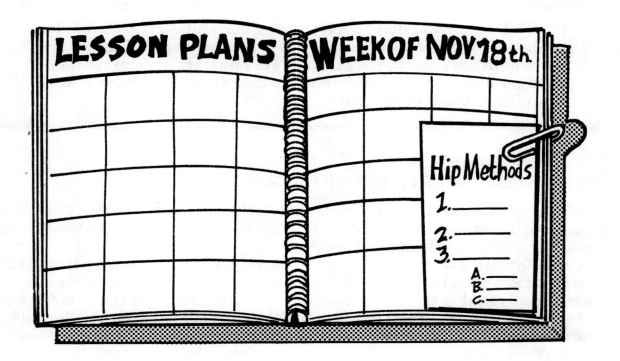

During my first HIP year, other teachers told me that I had a "good class." In truth, I had the usual number of behavior problems, but I wasn't alone; I was no longer the sole disciplinarian. Peer pressure served to bring students into line. As I initiated the program on a day-by-day basis, I could see a change in the entire class's attitude as the more difficult students began to shape up.

Misbehaving students discovered those seated around them did not want them in their station. It was not unusual for students, during the Class Meeting, to ask if they could vote a problem student out of their station. Misbehaving students were faced with the choice of obeying the rules or having to move to another station where they usually weren't wanted either. I seldom had to say a word because the students themselves got the word out for me.

HIP TIP: Do not let students vote others out of their stations. Only the teacher moves students.

I no longer was viewed as the "bad guy" in the room, meting out warnings, taking down names or keeping students after school. Instead, the rules were on the board. Students knew ahead of time what would happen when rules were disobeyed, because they understood the consequences of loss of Honor Points for a station and the ladder of discipline which would follow. They knew they would have to "face the music" at the Class Meeting.

One day a teacher from another state was directed to my classroom to observe. After walking about the room, talking with students and asking questions, she said to me, "You have a system that works. I would like to talk with you more about how you run this program." It was her comment and those from other teachers that inspired me to write this book.

FEELING GOOD ABOUT HIP

I strongly believe that feeling good should be part of a teacher's day, and that's the way I felt almost every day in my HIP classroom. I looked forward to going to school; the students, I could tell, enjoyed having me there.

In the next chapter you will find answers to a number of questions about the HIP classroom.

17

Questions and Answers

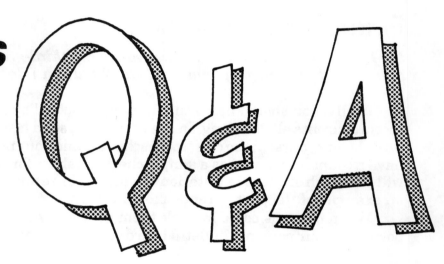

*E*veryone who hears about the HIP system invariably asks a lot of questions. Some of the most common are answered in this chapter, often with specific details for the best utilization of the system.

GENERAL QUESTIONS

Q. *Isn't this just one more way to use Behavior Modification in the classroom?*

A. First of all, let's define Behavior Modification. It is based upon the learning theory which rewards good behavior and punishes poor behavior in the belief that rewarded behavior will increase while punished behavior will decrease.

Technically, HIP could be considered Behavior Modification, but with a twist! At times, a single student is rewarded or punished, but the central focus of this system is to change student behavior through peer pressure. Rather than the teacher disciplining students, the desired behavior change is achieved through peer pressure within each station, thus freeing the teacher to do what he or she does best — teach!

Q. *I think the HIP plan sounds great but I'm not sure my principal would go along with it. How could I persuade him or her to let me use the system?*

A. Some schools use only one discipline program and you may not be free to change it. However, I would go to the principal saying you want to change to HIP as soon as possible. Also, I would ask the principal to read the HIP book. Even if you cannot make the change this year, emphasize that you wish to start a HIP classroom next year. You might even offer to have your room be a pilot test for the school. Most principals are open to suggestions, especially those which have been field-tested with proven results.

PARENTS IN THE CLASSROOM

Q. *I have thirty-one students this year in my third-grade classroom and no teacher's aide. I can't seem to get parents to help. What can I do?*

A. Ideally, you should begin the first day of school by asking for help and continue to recruit parents all year long. In the beginning, send home a general informational note introducing yourself, the classroom schedule and your needs. At the bottom of the sheet, have a coupon designed as a simple check-off sheet for parents. Tell your students you will give each student in a station ten points for returning the coupon. Page 121 shows an example of the part parents should return.

When coupons come in, look them over and make a tally sheet which should be posted on your personal bulletin board or kept in a folder at your desk for easy referral.

Q. *How can I best use these offers of help?*

A. Be prompt to send notes home to the parents emphasizing your appreciation that they are going to help you during the year.

For parents willing to help at home, let them know you will try to give them at least three days' notice before sending materials. This way you do not drop work into their laps unexpectedly.

PLEASE CLIP AND RETURN TO MRS. WILLIAMSON BY FRIDAY

– –

Mrs. Williamson: I'm willing to help in the classroom. I've circled the days I can come and I have checked in the box the time I can come.

(Circle days you can help and how many times per month)

1 2 3 4
Monday   Tuesday   Wednesday   Thursday   Friday

(Check in box the time you can come)
____8:00-9:00   Language Arts
____9:00-9:50   Reading
____10:00-10:50   Math
____10:50-11:15   Social Studies
____12:45-1:30   on Fridays for Art
____Other

I'm not able to help in the classroom but I'm willing to do the following:
____Go on field trips
____Grade papers at home
____Prepare art lessons
____Be a classroom speaker
____Other (Suggestions gratefully received.)
_____

_____

____I have special hobbies I could share with the class. Here are some ideas (or list your own): model airplane building or flying, bird raising, writing poetry, kite making, musical instrument playing. I could_____

_____

Mothers, fathers and grandparents are all welcome to take part in our classroom activities. As examples, fathers have talked to us about fishing, and grandparents have gone with us on field trips.

My name:_____

– –

For those parents coming to help in the school, send a note verifying their schedules and let them know you are looking forward to having them work in the classroom with you.

It is imperative you preplan their work. I found making lesson plans for parents is essential for a smooth-running room. *Example:* Mrs. R. came into my classroom each Monday at 9:30 and stayed for two hours. She did a variety of jobs such as preparing bulletin boards and putting them up each month, working on ongoing art projects and helping me when I worked with large groups of students.

I planned ahead each week for her Monday visit and I had a spot where I left her lesson plans. When I was busy, she waved and went to the shelf, read her work plan for the morning and began.

On one Monday the plans explained that she would be respraying thirty-three small chalkboards. The note indicated where she would find the necessary supplies and which students would help her. She was very efficient, worked quickly and did a fantastic job for me.

Q. *What is the best way to show my appreciation?*

A. In order to keep parents coming into my room on a weekly basis (at times, some fall by the wayside) I make a special effort to make them feel welcome, important and most of all, needed.

I try not to give parents only "grunt work" in my classroom, but rather to fit the jobs to their talents. Otherwise, they could get discouraged and no longer work. Of course, some work is repetitious and boring, but it has to be done. I try to have parents do different jobs in the room so they have some challenging and satisfying work along with the more menial tasks. Also, I am always open to suggestions from them as to easier ways to do jobs in the classroom.

HINT: Be aware that some parents may not have the education or experience to feel comfortable doing all jobs. In these cases, I ask them what they would enjoy doing and arrange my plans for them around their "comfort zones."

It is essential to be a good hostess to your parent helpers. I see my parents as guests in my classroom and I treat them as the very special people they are. Frequently, when they complete a project, I have the class stand and do a Three-Clap to show our classroom appreciation for their efforts.

In addition, on the back counter near the sink, I have a pretty tray for visitors to use. On it I keep colorful coffee mugs, a basket filled with herbal tea bags, a jar of instant coffee and a small "Hot Shot" pot® for heating water. I encourage the parents to stay in the room with me during recess to relax while we share a cup of tea. (Be sure local fire regulations permit you to have a hot pot in the classroom.)

At other times, if I don't have duty, I take them into the faculty lounge where I provide coffee and proudly introduce them to the other teachers.

In the spring I plan a luncheon held either in my home or at a restaurant where I treat my parent helpers. Here we socialize in a relaxed manner, as opposed to the often hectic working schedule in the classroom. We laugh together and enjoy an afternoon, not as teacher and parents but as friend with friends.

SPECIAL PROBLEMS WITH STUDENTS

Q. *I have a most active boy in my fifth-grade room. Even the students complain about his singing, burping and talking in class. He's driving us all crazy. What can I do?*

A. Set up your room according to the HIP model. Reread Chapter 9, Intermediate Class Meetings, and Chapter 10 on discipline procedures. Pay particular attention to the instructions for dealing with difficult students.

    If the behavior still does not change, purchase Dr. Paul Wood's tape, "How to Get Your Children to Do What You Want Them to Do." See Teacher Resources on page 131. I found what I needed in this tape. It tells how to demand in a loud, firm, no-nonsense voice what specific behavior you want from a particular problem student.

    I was also interested in Dr. Wood's theory that children are not hyperactive, only filled with anxiety — often as a result of problems in the home environment. Dr. Wood, a Los Angeles psychiatrist, describes how a teacher, by demanding specific behavior, can release the anxiety in a child who can then begin to function more effectively in the classroom.

Q. *I have several students this year who live in single-parent homes where their parents don't seem to care what their children do in the classroom. I get absolutely no backing from them. What can I do?*

A. I have had misbehaving students from single-parent homes and misbehaving students from homes with both parents. No matter what the home circumstances are, we teachers must set our own standards, enforce them and demand good behavior from students. We can do this even if we have no parental support. Remember that you are the most important person in this student's life, next to the parent. Arrange your room to function as a HIP classroom. I would have a private conference with the student and state clearly that he or she is part of the classroom and *will behave properly*.

    You could also discuss the problem in a Class Meeting. If the other students agree, the youngster could be placed on a contract and on any day when he or she does not lose points for the station, the station would receive a bonus of a specific number of points (for example, twenty points). I would set a time limit on the contract — such as one full month. In the Class Meeting, it would be helpful to let the other stations know that, at a later date, this student might be moved into their stations so it is vital that they also encourage the student to behave as desired.

Q. *In my classroom I have a ten-year-old girl who is constantly demanding my attention. Within the first five minutes after she arrives, she comes up to me at least three times, either telling me "home stories" or asking such questions as where she can find a ruler. She knows perfectly well where they are kept. How can I get her to be less demanding of my time and attention?*

A. I've had similar situations in my classroom. For example, Troy was a very nervous child and talked all day long. From his records, I saw this had been a continuing problem for him in school. When I had the school counselor interview Troy, he noted the same behavior. Here are the steps I took:

1. I met privately with Troy and we discussed his constant need to talk to me, even in the middle of a lesson. We agreed that some questions were important because they had to do with his seatwork. However, I also made it very clear that when he could control his need to talk to me and to others, he would have more time to listen, get directions and do his seatwork too, so he would not have homework each night. We mutually agreed that he could come up to me seven times a day and either ask or tell me something. He understood that he should pick out the seven most important things he needed to say and he could not interrupt a lesson.

2. Each morning, I wrote a small contract on the chalkboard by writing his name and the numbers from one to seven. Each time he came up, I'd "X" out the appropriate number.

3. On some of his daily visits, I reminded him how important his questions were and that I was so pleased with how selective he was becoming in picking out the most important things to discuss.

Chalkboard →

Chalk and Chalk tray

Eraser →

Troy
X̶ X̶ X̶ 3
4 5 6

Within three weeks, Troy came to me and said, "I'm doing better, aren't I?" I praised him, pointing out that the day before he'd used only five of his contract numbers. We agreed that the following week we should go for five talking times each day. Eventually, we went to three and finally were able to discontinue the contract altogether.

Caution: You should mark off the numbers. At first I felt Troy should, but I soon noticed he made a game of running up, talking to me, then dashing over and making a big production of finding an eraser and very slowly erasing a tiny number.

Q. *I have an unusually high number of active students in my fourth-grade class this year. They have trouble sitting for very long in the classroom to do their work. What can I do to settle them down?*

A. The physical education program we use in our classroom is a natural for burning off excess energy. In order to add zest to my program, I purchased jump ropes and hoops for each student. Also, I was able to buy a large parachute from a surplus store to use as a group activity. (Check with your principal before buying the parachute to see if it must be sprayed with fire retardant and then kept secure in a metal can in the classroom so students will not use it as a tent and suffocate themselves).

I sometimes use the jump ropes after an unusually long math lesson when the students frequently become very fidgety. I hand them each a jump rope and we go outside and do easy warm up exercises for a few minutes. Then we jump "hot peppers" for another minute or so. Later, I ask the students to line up at one end of the blacktop with their ropes ready. At my signal, they skip rope down to the end of the blacktop. After a long drink, they return to the classroom ready to settle down again. All of this takes less than ten minutes to accomplish. For additional ideas on P.E. activities, see page 131 in Teacher Resources.

Our final question is of importance not only to new teachers but, at times, to each of us.

Q. *This is my first year of teaching and I feel so ineffective and stressed out. How can HIP help me become the strong teacher I dreamed I would be?*

A. The HIP system is designed to make you, the teacher, a take-charge person. As Chairman of the Board, you are in charge, but you may need to practice enhancing your self-image as an effective teacher. An excellent way is through affirmations. An affirmation is simply a strong positive statement which you repeat to yourself. Make your own affirmations and put them on cards to look at each morning, or make affirmation tapes to listen to while driving to school each morning. Some examples are:
- I am a take-charge teacher.
- Students are eager to learn what I have to share.
- I am a gifted teacher who cares about my students.
- My students see me as a positive teacher.
- I am confident, serene and happy today.

Affirmations must be written in a positive manner; never use the word *don't*. For instance, instead of saying, "Misbehaving students don't get me down," say, "I competently and calmly deal with misbehaving students."

There is a large variety of motivational tapes which will help you become the strong teacher you dreamed of in college. Perhaps the teachers at your school would like to develop a lending library of such tapes in your teachers' lounge. On page 131 in Teacher Resources, you'll find information about tapes and an outstanding workbook to help you reduce stress so you'll be well on your way to becoming a successful teacher.

CHAPTER 3

<u>Marva Collins' Way</u>
by Marva Collins and Civia Tamarkin
Order from:
Dynamic Teaching Company
P. O. Box 276711
Sacramento, CA 95827
(916) 351-1912

CHAPTER 4

<u>101 Ways to Put Pizazz into Your
Teaching</u>, page 55
by Bonnie Williamson
Order from:
Dynamic Teaching Company
P. O. Box 276711
Sacramento, CA 95827
(916) 351-1912

CHAPTER 7

<u>A First-Year Teacher's Guidebook for
Success</u>, pages 95-102
by Bonnie Williamson
Order from:
Dynamic Teaching Company
P. O. Box 276711
Sacramento, CA 95827
(916) 351-1912

CHAPTER 9

<u>Maintaining Sanity in the Classroom</u>
by Rudolph Dreikurs
Published by Harper, 1971
New York, NY 10022

CHAPTER 10

<u>Positive Classroom Discipline</u>
Chapter 18
by Fredric H. Jones
Order from:
Dynamic Teaching Company
P. O. Box 276711
Sacramento, CA 95827
(916) 351-1912

<u>The Hmong: Yesterday and Today</u>
<u>Iu Mien: Tradition and Change</u>
<u>The Ethnic Lao: Who are They?</u>
by Pat Moore-Howard
Order from:
Pat Moore-Howard
2731 Sutterville Road
Sacramento, CA 95820
Telephone: (916) 451-2477

Three outstanding books written
by a mentor teacher who has travelled
to the Far East to study these cul-
tures. A MUST READ resource for all
teachers working with children from
these countries.

CHAPTER 11

Awesome Elementary School P.E.
Activities and P.E. Units For Primary
Teachers
by Cliff Carnes
Order from:
   Dynamic Teaching Company
   P. O. Box 276711
   Sacramento, CA 95827
   (916) 351-1912

CHAPTER 13

If You're Trying to Teach Kids How to
Write, You've Gotta Have This Book!
by Marjorie Frank
Order from:
   Dynamic Teaching Company
   P. O. Box 276711
   Sacramento, CA 95827
   (916) 351-1912

MULTIPLICATION TABLES

1 X 1 = 1	2 X 1 = 2	3 X 1 = 3
1 X 2 = 2	2 X 2 = 4	3 X 2 = 6
1 X 3 = 3	2 X 3 = 6	3 X 3 = 9
1 X 4 = 4	2 X 4 = 8	3 X 4 = 12
1 X 5 = 5	2 X 5 = 10	3 X 5 = 15
1 X 6 = 6	2 X 6 = 12	3 X 6 = 18
1 X 7 = 7	2 X 7 = 14	3 X 7 = 21
1 X 8 = 8	2 X 8 = 16	3 X 8 = 24
1 X 9 = 9	2 X 9 = 18	3 X 9 = 27
1 X 10 = 10	2 X 10 = 20	3 X 10 = 30
1 X 11 = 11	2 X 11 = 22	3 X 11 = 33
1 X 12 = 12	2 X 12 = 24	3 X 12 = 36

4 X 1 = 4	5 X 1 = 5	6 X 1 = 6
4 X 2 = 8	5 X 2 = 10	6 X 2 = 12
4 X 3 = 12	5 X 3 = 15	6 X 3 = 18
4 X 4 = 16	5 X 4 = 20	6 X 4 = 24
4 X 5 = 20	5 X 5 = 25	6 X 5 = 30
4 X 6 = 24	5 X 6 = 30	6 X 6 = 36
4 X 7 = 28	5 X 7 = 35	6 X 7 = 42
4 X 8 = 32	5 X 8 = 40	6 X 8 = 48
4 X 9 = 36	5 X 9 = 45	6 X 9 = 54
4 X 10 = 40	5 X 10 = 50	6 X 10 = 60
4 X 11 = 44	5 X 11 = 55	6 X 11 = 66
4 X 12 = 48	5 X 12 = 60	6 X 12 = 72

7 X 1 = 7	8 X 1 = 8	9 X 1 = 9
7 X 2 = 14	8 X 2 = 16	9 X 2 = 18
7 X 3 = 21	8 X 3 = 24	9 X 3 = 27
7 X 4 = 28	8 X 4 = 32	9 X 4 = 36
7 X 5 = 35	8 X 5 = 40	9 X 5 = 45
7 X 6 = 42	8 X 6 = 48	9 X 6 = 54
7 X 7 = 49	8 X 7 = 56	9 X 7 = 63
7 X 8 = 56	8 X 8 = 64	9 X 8 = 72
7 X 9 = 63	8 X 9 = 72	9 X 9 = 81
7 X 10 = 70	8 X 10 = 80	9 X 10 = 90
7 X 11 = 77	8 X 11 = 88	9 X 11 = 99
7 X 12 = 84	8 X 12 = 96	9 X 12 = 108

10 X 1 = 10	11 X 1 = 11	12 X 1 = 12
10 X 2 = 20	11 X 2 = 22	12 X 2 = 24
10 X 3 = 30	11 X 3 = 33	12 X 3 = 36
10 X 4 = 40	11 X 4 = 44	12 X 4 = 48
10 X 5 = 50	11 X 5 = 55	12 X 5 = 60
10 X 6 = 60	11 X 6 = 66	12 X 6 = 72
10 X 7 = 70	11 X 7 = 77	12 X 7 = 84
10 X 8 = 80	11 X 8 = 88	12 X 8 = 96
10 X 9 = 90	11 X 9 = 99	12 X 9 = 108
10 X 10 = 100	11 X 10 = 110	12 X 10 = 120
10 X 11 = 110	11 X 11 = 121	12 X 11 = 132
10 X 12 = 120	11 X 12 = 132	12 X 12 = 144

Books for Stress Reduction and Self-Improvement

The Relaxation & Stress- Reduction Workbook
by Davis, Eshelman and McKay
Order from:
New Harbinger Publications
5674 Shattuck Avenue
Oakland, CA 94609

Recreating Your Self (affirmation use)
by Nancy J. Napier
Order from:
W. W. Norton & Company, Inc.
500 Fifth Avenue
New York, NY 10110

Tapes for Stress Reduction

"Understanding Stress and Learning to Relax"
by Paul Wood
Order from:
Dr. Paul Wood
18800 Main Street, Suite 207
Huntington, Beach, CA 92648
(714) 842-0048

"Increased Relaxation with Relaxed Breathing"
by Dr. Reneau Peurifoy
Order from:
LifeSkills Publications/Tapes
P. O. Box 7915
Citrus Heights, CA 95621
(916) 366-9444

CHAPTER 15

Free Things for Teachers
by Susan Osborn
Order from:
Dynamic Teaching Company
P. O. Box 276711
Sacramento, CA 95827
(916) 351-1912

For additional information on how to raise funds for your classroom see:
A First-Year Teacher's Guidebook for Success, p. 153
by Bonnie Williamson
Order from:
Dynamic Teaching Company
P. O. Box 276711
Sacramento, CA 95827
(916) 351-1912

CHAPTER 17

Tape — "How to Get Your Children to Do What You Want Them to Do"
by Paul Wood
Order from:
Dr. Paul Wood
18800 Main Street, Suite 207
Huntington Beach, CA 92648

Awesome Elementary School P.E Activities and P.E. Units For Primary Teachers
by Cliff Carnes
Order from:
Dynamic Teaching Company
P. O. Box 276711
Sacramento, CA 95827
(916) 351-1912

Accessories, chairman's, 8-9
Affirmations for strong self-image, 127
Anecdotal records, importance of, 75, 77
Attention, ways teacher gains, 7, 88
Bailiff, 86, 91, 107
Behavior problems, 71-78, 108
    anxiety as cause, 124
    class discussion of, 124-125
    contracts for, 75, 124-125
    from single-parent homes, 124-125
    importance of home contact, 75-76
    improvement acknowledgement, 76,
        125-126
    reasons for, 66
Carpet, 37
Chairman of the Board, teacher as, 3, 8
Chairman-of-the-Board table, 8
Choice for failure or smartness, 17-22
Class Meetings, intermediate, 54, 65-70
    agenda, importance of, 65-67
    benefits to students, 70
    compliments, 67
    consequences or punishment, 69,
        124-125
    lack of time for, 105-107
    preparation for, 67
    responsibilities of teacher, 69
    rules & procedures, 67-68
    sample, 68-69
Class Meeting, primary, 57-64, 115
    apologies for problem behavior, 61-62
    benefits to students, 62-63
    compliments, 60
    conducting of, 59-64
    feelings discussion, 61
    feelings shown by teacher, 64
    planning ahead for, 59
    problem discussion, 60-63
    responsibilities of teacher, 63-64
    rules and procedures, 59, 62
    students who hurt others, 62
    timing during the day, 58
    use of timer, 60
    vulgar name problems, 11, 64

Classroom arrangement
    Cooperative Learning positions, 6-7
    kindergarten, 10
    stations, 5-6
    Total Language, 6-7
Classroom family, 11
Classroom management system, 2-3
Classroom supplies/accessories, 8-9
Competitive spirit, 23
Complaints, intermediate & primary, 57
Consecutive numbers, primary, 92-93
Consequences, 66, 68, 69
Contract seeking good behavior, 124-125
Counting the stars, 103
Custodian, source of help, 25
Daily journal, 21, 97-98
Desk name tags, 23-24
Discipline, 71-78
    after-school suspension, 78
    behavior contracts, 75
    in-house suspension, 77
    ladder, 71
    limit setting, intermediate, 73
    sending students to the office, 77
    suspension from school, 77
    teacher-to-teacher suspension, 78
    use in P.E., intermediate, 73, 82
Early-late schedule, 103
Empty desk, 24
Enthusiasm and feeling good, 118
Facilitator, teacher as, 3, 54, 66, 69
Feelings, 11-14, 61, 64, 66, 85, 89, 108,
    118
Finger snapping, 26, 102
Flexibility, importance of, 105-107
Graphing, "success/failure," 17-18
Hand signals, 66
(HIP) Honor Incentive Point system
    definition, 1-4
    HIP chart, 25-27, 47, 108
    Compared to Behavior Modification,
      119
    Reactions to, by author, 115-118
      intermediate students, 114-115

parents, 114-115
primary students, 113-114
split class, 115
TIPS for Subs, 28
Honor Points, 107-108, 117
Job assignments, intermediate, 37-42
kindergarten, 10, 37
primary, 34-37
Job committees, monthly terms, 47
Job Meetings, 33
committee system, 46-47
intermediate, 46-47
primary, 43-45, 113
Job nominations and voting, 43-44
Job nominations by proxy, 45
Jobs, scheduling for least disruption, 36
Journals
preparation as art activity, 97-98
read as part of Sharing, 97-98
written by students, 21, 97-98
Judge, teacher as, 3, 63
Ladder of discipline, 71, 117
Logical consequences, 66
Loyalty of class toward teacher, 106
Mistaken behavior, 66
Model for class activities, teacher as, 67, 86, 96
Monday, importance in HIP system, 33-34
Money matters, 109-111
Money-raising ideas, 109-111
door-to-door selling discouraged, 111
Morale problems, 73
Multiplication fact chart, 97
Multiplication facts competition, 96-97
Multiplication Folder, intermediate, 94-97
as art activity, 94-95
Name calling, 11, 64
Non-English-speaking parents, 76
Number Book, 93
as art activity, 93
as number competition, 93
Parade, primary, Tell Time, 87-88

Parent help, 103, 120-123
coupon solicitation for, 120-122
preplanned work for, 122
giving thanks for, 103, 109, 122-123
Parent table, 9
Peer pressure, 3, 28, 31, 62, 75 108, 116
and seating arrangements, 19-20
Physical education (P.E.), 79-82
activity favorites, intermediate, 82
co-captains, primary, 80
committee approach, intermediate, 82
for enforcing classroom discipline, 82
"out of circulation," 73
peer tutoring, primary, 82
plan ahead before September, 79
team captain selection, primary, 80-81
team names, primary, 81
walking the Perimeter, 71-73
warm-up activities, intermediate, 82
way to calm down active students, 126-127
Play money, intermediate level, 41
Point count, 26, 47-48
Point payoffs, 31-42
field trips, 41-42
Point recording, 30-32, 33, 107-108
Point system, 25-32
Points, choosing to lose, 31
Points, ways to earn, 27-30
Prep time, 98
President and/or vice president, intermediate
jobs modeled by teacher, 54
responsibilities, 53-54, 86-87, 91-92, 96
station moves, 56
President/vice president, primary, 113-114
responsibilities, 51-53
station moves, 50-51
Presidential election, intermediate, 55-56
Presidential election, primary, 49-50
leadership qualities, 49-50

preparation for, 50
problem students addressed, 50
students encouraged to run for, 50
Presidential election, U.S. national, 49
Principal's permission for HIP use, 120
Punishment, 62, 66, 69
Relaxation break for teacher, 87, 100
Reporting, 16, 58, 65
Respect, interpersonal, 3, 67-68
Responsibility for learning, 17
shared, teacher & students, 3, 47
Role playing, 12-14
Rules, classroom
benefits, 15
home, 11
intermediate classroom, 17
primary classroom, 15-16
selection by students & teacher, 14-15
ways to implement, 14
School counselor, 75
Seat assignments, 23-24
Self-esteem, 63, 114
Sharing, intermediate, 54, 88-92, 98
SOS, student-out-of-station, 73-74
Special problems with students, 124-127
Star Achievers, 103-104
Star Box, 102
Star Cards, 101-104
Star prizes, 104
Station, definition, 25
Stations, naming, 25-26
Staying in school, 17-22
Stress reduction, 100, 127-28
Student elections, 43-44
Student help, 109
Students' classroom responsibility, 47
Supportive leader, teacher as, 3
Suspension, 77-78
Talking out in class, 12-13
Tattling, 16, 58
Tell Time, 83-87, 90-92
primary, 85
Telling the News, 83-92, 105
preparing students for, 86

primary parade, 87-88
Thanks, help/good work, 25, 103, 109, 122-123
Threats, students against peers, 106
Three-Clap, 26, 72, 102
Time & money management, 105-112
Time out for teacher, 91-93, 98-100, 108
Total classroom committees, 38-41
Total Language Activity Program, 1, 97-98
Van Dyke, Marie, 2
Walking the Perimeter, 62, 71-73, 108
Weekly auction, 41
Winner Assemblies, 104
Witnesses to discipline problems, 64, 68